CITY MAKING IN PARADISE

CITY MAKING

MIKE HARCOURT

& KEN CAMERON

with SEAN ROSSITER

IN PARADISE

Nine Decisions That

Saved Vancouver

DOUGLAS & MCINTYRE

VANCOUVER/TORONTO

Douglas & McIntyre Ltd.
2323 Quebec Street, Suite 201
Vancouver, British Columbia
Canada V5T 4S7
www.douglas-mcintyre.com

Library and Archives Canada Cataloguing in Publication
Harcourt, Michael, 1943–
City making in paradise : nine decisions that saved
Vancouver / Mike Harcourt & Ken Cameron ; with Sean Rossiter.
Includes index.

ISBN 978-1-55365-257-1

1. Regional planning—British Columbia—Vancouver Metropolitan
Area—History.   2. Regional planning—British Columbia—Vancouver
Metropolitan Area—Citizen participation—History.   3. Urban
policy—British Columbia—History.   4. Quality of life—British
Columbia—Vancouver Metropolitan Area.   5. Sustainable development—
British Columbia—Vancouver Metropolitan Area.   6. Vancouver
Metropolitan Area (B.C.)—History.   I. Rossiter, Sean, 1946–
II. Cameron, Ken (Kenneth Duncan)   III. Title.

HT395.C33V3542 2007   307.1'160971133   C2007-902066-6

Copy editing by Iva Cheung
Cover and text design by Naomi MacDougall
Cover photographs by Naomi MacDougall
Maps by Eric Leinberger
Printed and bound in Canada by Friesens
Printed on acid-free paper that is forest friendly (100% post-
consumer recycled paper) and has been processed chlorine free.

We gratefully acknowledge the financial support of the Canada Council for the Arts, the Brit-
ish Columbia Arts Council, the Province of British Columbia through the Book Publishing Tax
Credit, and the Government of Canada through the Book Publishing Industry Development
Program (BPIDP) for our publishing activities.

Contents

Preface and Dedication

CITY MAKING IN PARADISE was conceived in the fall of 2004 by Mike Harcourt and Ken Cameron over coffee at Cuppa Joe's in Jericho Village on Vancouver's west side.

After a thirty-year political career that had taken him from a storefront law office through the mayor of Vancouver's chair to the premiership of British Columbia, Harcourt had donned the persona of "recovering politician" after his retirement in 1996. He had returned to his first love—studying how cities work to protect the social, economic and physical well-being of all their citizens. His post-politics roles had included serving on the boards of the Vancouver Airport Authority, the Vancouver Port Authority and the B.C. Treaty Commission and an appointment to the University of British Columbia's Liu Centre for the Study of Global Issues. He was soon to be tapped by the Paul Martin government to chair the prime minister's task force on cities and communities and to co-chair the national advisory committee on Canada's preparations to host the third United Nations World Urban Forum in Vancouver in June 2006. Harcourt was recovering in an even more profound and challenging way, too. On November 30, 2002, he had suffered a severe spinal cord injury in a fall from the deck at his summer home on North Pender Island.

Ken Cameron had been born and raised in Vancouver and was living in the home he grew up in. He had spent enough time in other major Canadian cities, though, to know that Vancouver was where he wanted to live and die. In a stint with the Ontario government after his graduation from the UBC School of Community and Regional Planning in 1970, Cameron had performed a number of roles at the interface between politics and government, including serving as executive assistant to Ontario Treasurer John White and executive director of the Royal Commission on Metropolitan Toronto headed by former Ontario premier John Robarts. After returning to Vancouver in 1978, Cameron served in senior planning and management positions with the City of New Westminster and the Greater Vancouver Regional District (GVRD), ultimately as manager of policy and planning with responsibility for managing air quality and planning for regional growth, including issues regarding water supply, liquid waste and solid waste. By September 2004, he concluded he had done everything he could within the system to overcome the wheel-spinning and leadership deficit at the regional level and accepted a job as chief executive officer of the provincial Homeowner Protection Office. He made it a condition of his appointment that he be able to remain professionally involved in contributing to the region's future from outside the GVRD organization.

Harcourt and Cameron had enjoyed a respectful relationship and supportive collaboration throughout their careers, but their first opportunity to work closely together unfolded through their involvement in the International Centre for Sustainable Cities (ICSC), a Vancouver-based non-governmental organization dedicated to advancing urban sustainability through demonstration projects at home and in developing countries. Cameron had been involved in founding the organization in 1993 as part of the Mulroney government's Green Plan and had served on its board continuously, including a term as its chair. When Harcourt became available after 1996, Cameron and ICSC's CEO, Nola-Kate Seymoar, recruited him to serve on the board, including a term as chair and, ultimately, as honorary chair.

The early years of this decade provided two opportunities for Greater Vancouver's developing mass of expertise in urban sustainability to show its strength—citiesPLUS and the World Urban Forum. Through ICSC, Cameron and Harcourt were close collaborators in both.

citiesPLUS was Canada's entry in the International Gas Union's competition for a hundred-year sustainable urban system design plans. The GVRD, through Cameron, partnered with the Sheltair Group through Sebastian Moffatt, to submit a successful bid to the Canadian Gas Association for the right to represent Canada in this competition. This set the stage for a broader partnership, including ICSC and UBC, through the Liu Centre, to prepare the submission. The project drew in a remarkable range of participants from within Greater Vancouver and across Canada. Harcourt served as vice-chair of the advisory committee, and Cameron served as regional team leader in the project, which produced a submission that showed how Greater Vancouver could vastly increase its sustainability and reduce its ecological footprint without compromising its economy or its quality of life. (See www.citiesplus.ca)

Harcourt participated enthusiastically in the early stages of preparing the submission, travelling to Japan for preliminary meetings and actively coaching the project team. His accident abruptly curtailed his involvement, but it provided strong motivation for the project team to win the competition on his behalf. Moffatt, Seymoar and Cameron travelled to Tokyo in June

2003 to present the project to the jury of international sustainability experts. Their entry won gold prize.

The idea of hosting the UN's third World Urban Forum was hatched at an Environment Canada consultation meeting in February 2002 leading up to the Earth Summit in Johannesburg that August. Peter Oberlander—founder of UBC's school of planning and a former federal deputy minister of State for Urban Affairs—Seymoar and Cameron conceived the idea as a way of focussing local and world attention on Greater Vancouver's achievements and challenges while commemorating the thirtieth anniversary of the landmark UN-Habitat conference, held in Vancouver in 1976. Harcourt enlisted in the scheme, promoting it through his contacts in Prime Minister Jean Chrétien's office. Federal public servants were not receptive to the idea, and a declaration of Canada's offer to host the forum was not included in the draft of the prime minister's speech when he left Ottawa for Johannesburg. Oberlander, Harcourt and Cameron worked their contacts while Chrétien's party was en route, and the prime minister issued the invitation to the UN before those assembled for the Earth Summit not once but twice.

Harcourt and Cameron's initial idea at Cuppa Joe's was for a book that could be a resource for people attending the forum. In their discussions, however, they soon identified a much more important purpose. They wanted to show as wide a readership as possible the important choices that had been made in the Greater Vancouver region and the consequences of those choices. By focussing on key decisions and the people involved in making them, the book would carry the strong message that regional leadership is critical if Greater Vancouver is to continue to enjoy its reputation as one of the world's most livable cities. They decided to enlist a third collaborator, Sean Rossiter, a writer specializing in architecture and urban affairs who had covered city politics for thirteen years in his award-winning *Vancouver* magazine column, "Twelfth & Cambie."

City Making in Paradise is a joint project. Parts of it were drafted by Harcourt and Cameron, the rest by Rossiter. The final product is the result of many long and lively discussions to give shape to information derived from interviews or dredged from memory. The book expresses our collective perspective on events in which we were intimately involved, as actors or commentators. To promote the smoothest possible reading experience, we have made the decision to refer to ourselves in the third person throughout.

IN WRITING *City Making in Paradise,* we became aware that Walter Hardwick's presence permeated many of the decisions we identified as being critical to the Greater Vancouver region's livability. As a professor of geography at UBC, Hardwick shaped the perspectives of countless students who would later assume leadership positions in Greater Vancouver and elsewhere. A co-founder of The Electors' Action Movement (TEAM), Hardwick had served one term on Vancouver city council before that group swept into power in Vancouver in 1972. As a councillor, he oversaw planning for the transformation of the south shore of False Creek, fulfilling his long-held vision for the area and demonstrating how inner-city industrial areas could become self-sufficient, livable communities without creating the additional burden on the regional transportation system that comes from suburban growth. As a researcher, Hardwick led the Vancouver Urban Futures Project, an in-depth survey of public values published in 1974 that informed the first Livable Region Proposals, and he repeated that survey in 1989–90 as part of the GVRD's Choosing Our Future project to ground-test public attitudes after the economic shocks of the early 1980s. In the process, he uncovered deep truths about the attitudes of Greater Vancouver residents towards their region that would guide decision making for decades. In the intervening years, Hardwick served as provincial deputy minister for Education, Science and Technology and was responsible for establishing the Open Learning Institute and the Knowledge Network, serving as chair of the latter. In the course of his career, he demonstrated always his belief in the liberating influence of knowledge on the progression of the human spirit, collectively and individually.

At Hardwick's memorial service in August 2005, Ken Cameron offered these words: "Walter Hardwick was a master craftsman in the development of leaders and leadership. He did it not only by teaching, but as importantly by showing, doing and telling—by leading himself." It is therefore appropriate that this book about leadership in city making is dedicated to his memory.

MIKE HARCOURT
KEN CAMERON
SEAN ROSSITER

Vancouver, British Columbia
March 3, 2007

CITY MAKING IN PARADISE

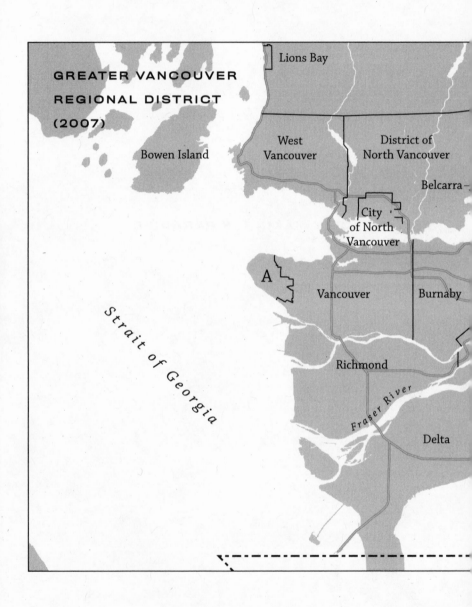

GREATER VANCOUVER
REGIONAL DISTRICT
(2007)

Lions Bay

Bowen Island

West
Vancouver

District of
North Vancouver

Belcarra

City
of North
Vancouver

A

Vancouver

Burnaby

Strait of Georgia

Richmond

Fraser River

Delta

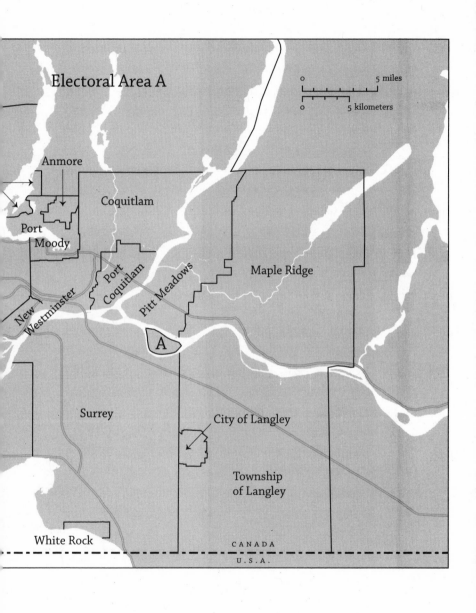

Electoral Area A

5 miles
5 kilometers

Anmore

Coquitlam

Port
Moody

Port
Coquitlam

Pitt Meadows

New
Westminster

Maple Ridge

A

Surrey

City of Langley

Township
of Langley

White Rock

CANADA
U.S.A.

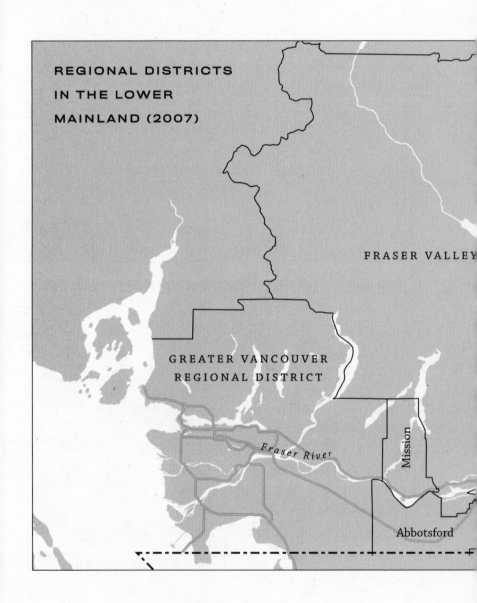

REGIONAL DISTRICTS
IN THE LOWER
MAINLAND (2007)

FRASER VALLEY

GREATER VANCOUVER
REGIONAL DISTRICT

Mission

Fraser River

Abbotsford

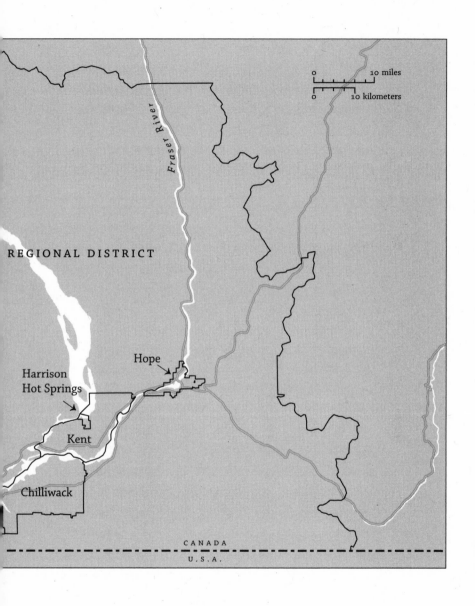

Introduction

HALF OF THE world's 6 billion people and 80 per cent of Canada's population currently live in cities. Virtually all of the next 2.5 billion people predicted to populate the world by 2025 will live in cities. The economic, social and political affairs of humanity are increasingly understood as taking place within and between systems of cities rather than nations. Our success at achieving national and international human security and development goals will be largely a function of our ability to plan and manage the development of cities.

Vancouver appears at or close to the top of nearly every international list of the best places to live. Those chronicling its success at following a path different from that of most other urban regions have even coined a term, "Vancouverism," to describe the philosophies and approaches observable here: multiple-use, high-density core areas; a transit-focussed and auto-restrained transportation system; exquisite urban design to echo a spectacular natural setting; and a peaceful, tolerant multicultural population. In short, a place that gets it right, most of the time.

The place we now know as the Greater Vancouver region has been a paradise, an ideal place for human habitation, from time immemorial. For at least ten thousand years before the tentacles of European civilization reached the Salish Sea in the eighteenth century, Coast Salish Aboriginal groups such as the Squamish, the Katzie, the Musqueam, the Tsleil-Waututh, the Stó:lō and the Tsawwassen thrived in the area. The temperate climate and abundance of life-supporting flora and fauna produced enough surpluses in time and energy to support a spiritually rich and creative culture, inspired by the sacred nature of the creatures of the sea, sky and land: the killer whale, the raven and above all the salmon, in such numbers that rivers would nearly overflow their banks.

The promise of the place astounded the first Europeans to visit. In 1792 Captain George Vancouver wrote, "To describe the beauty of this region will, on some occasion, be a very grateful task to the pen."

The three most important events to affect the region in the nineteenth century were all acts of conscious city making. The first was the decision by Colonel Richard Moody of the Royal Engineers to establish the City of New Westminster in 1854 as the capital for the Crown colony of British Columbia. Colonel Moody selected the site on the north shore of the Fraser River because of its proximity to river and ocean transportation and its elevated state behind the natural barrier of the river, which provided the best prospects for detecting and repelling a potential attack by invading Americans. In 1866 the city was designated as the capital of the combined colonies of British Columbia and Vancouver Island, only to lose this status to Victoria a few years later. (The governor preferred to live in Victoria, and the New Westminster legislators were inebriated at the time of the vote, two not unrelated events.) The second event was the decision of the Canadian Pacific Railway to move the intended location of the railway's Pacific tidewater terminus ten miles west from the initial choice at Port Moody to the Granville townsite, a decision that deftly doused the paper fortunes of land speculators at Port Moody so that the profits of land speculation around the terminus could be enjoyed by the CPR itself. From the beginning, the urban region that was to become known as Greater Vancouver was a multi-centred place. The third event was the first decision of the Vancouver city council, after its establishment in 1886, to ask the government of Canada to turn over the reserve adjacent to the townsite for park use as what would become Stanley Park. It represented a vision that the city would always be connected to the wilderness out of which it was built.

For the first half of the twentieth century, the Vancouver region evolved modestly and unremarkably. Vancouver proper became the dominant centre, building on its tidewater terminal functions to become the service centre for British Columbia's resource-rich economy. After losing its status as a capital city to Victoria, New Westminster found a new role as the market centre for the thriving farmers and fishers of the Fraser River valley. Residents of the region were quietly smug about their good fortune in living in such a benign location, somewhat insulated from the great disasters—two world wars and a depression—that dominated world attention.

Local governments were established as needed, in accordance with British Columbia's tradition of supporting local institutions where populations desired them. In 1951, there were thirteen municipalities in what is now Greater Vancouver, with a total population of 562,000. By 1971 there were 1,028,000 souls living in fifteen municipalities. Today, Greater Vancouver comprises twenty-one municipalities with a combined population of 2,181,000 people—a four-fold increase in less than sixty years.

Although these municipalities fostered strong communities of people loyal to their places, their built forms were underwhelming. Commentators on urbanity in the 1960s were fond of describing Greater Vancouver as "a setting in search of a city." A ubiquitous form of single-family housing was the "Vancouver Special"—two levels of frame construction built on a concrete slab with an attached garage, designed to be easily converted into illegal suites. Upon his arrival in Vancouver from Toronto in 1973 as the City of Vancouver's director of planning, Ray Spaxman was heard to muse whether Vancouver aspired to be "more than a logger's long weekend." There were no Class A office buildings outside of the City of Vancouver until 1978, when the B.C. Telephone Company (now Telus) opened its new head office building in Burnaby, just a few feet outside the Vancouver boundary.

By the first few years of the twenty-first century, all that had changed. Greater Vancouver consistently ranked high among the world's cities because of its clean environment, range of housing choices, lively but safe streets, outstanding outdoor recreation opportunities, diverse but peaceful population and excellent public services. The region won the UN-Habitat 2002 Dubai Award for the quality of its planning and gold prize in the International Gas Union's 2003 competition for a hundred-year urban sustainability plans for its innovative citiesPLUS project. Along with Paris, San Francisco and Sydney, Vancouver was listed as a "resort city," a place where the rich and famous own homes for their recreational use.

Greater Vancouver began to play a role in the international consideration of the problems of human settlements by hosting the UN-Habitat conference in 1976. The conference led to the establishment of UN-Habitat, which evolved into a full-fledged UN program in 2002. A key element of UN-Habitat's program is to stimulate dialogue involving the public and private sectors and civil society through biennial World Urban Forums. When the third World Urban Forum convened in Vancouver in 2006, there was a sense that the region had discovered many of the secrets of successful urban settlement.

City Making in Paradise tells the stories of nine of the regional decisions made since 1945 that contributed to the transformation of Greater Vancouver into one of the world's most livable cities. These are not the only stories, but they are among the most important ones. With one exception, they focus on specific decisions made at a particular time and place. The exception is our examination of the role of the provincial government of British Columbia, which has followed, reasonably consistently, a constructive and enabling approach to the efforts of local government to create an outstanding urban region.

What do we mean by the word "city"? In *City Making in Paradise*, the term refers to the entity where most of the urban area's transactions and trips take place daily. It encompasses the area's markets for labour, housing, transportation and commerce. It is an organic entity that grows and changes in response to internal and external influences. It has different parts that have different functions, all essential to the growth and prosperity of the whole.

There was a time—in Greater Vancouver and elsewhere—when the city in this organic form was encompassed within its political boundaries. This was the case with both New Westminster and the City of Vancouver itself. When separate suburban municipalities such as South Vancouver and Point Grey came into being, common sense often led to their integration, maintaining the fit between the organic city and the political one. But that comfortable evolutionary pattern was shattered throughout North America after World War II by a combination of rapid suburban growth and widespread use of the automobile, which led to the establishment of more distant suburbs with their own local governments.

Vancouver as a city in these terms extends well beyond the forty-four square miles of territory lying west of Boundary Road. It includes all of the area within Statistics Canada's Vancouver Census Metropolitan Area, which coincides with the boundaries of the Greater Vancouver Regional District (GVRD).

The lack of fit between the organic city or urban region and its political institutions has bedevilled rational decision making in urban regions since the end of World War II. Responses elsewhere have included the formation of metropolitan governments in Toronto

in 1953 and Winnipeg in 1959, as well as later merg-
ers to create amalgamated "megacities" in Winnipeg,
Toronto, Ottawa, Montreal and Halifax. *City Making
in Paradise* chronicles the efforts of responsible, coura-
geous leaders in Greater Vancouver to chart and follow
a course that would allow the region to grow into a
major metropolis while not only retaining its diverse
patchwork of local jurisdictions but also enhancing,
rather than degrading, its natural and human heritage.

Greater Vancouver stories played out on a landscape
unique in more ways than one. Every province except
British Columbia had established rural local governments and, in many cases, county governments from
their earliest days. In British Columbia, more than 95
per cent of the land base was essentially under colonial
administration by the provincial government until
regional districts were created in the 1960s, and more
than 90 per cent of the province's land is still owned
by the Crown. Local municipalities are created in British Columbia only if citizens express their support
for such a move. Politically, then, local municipalities
must be respected as the product and the embodiment
of local democracy. Municipalities established in this
way have much greater legitimacy than those established by the stroke of a colonial governor's pen.

On this landscape grew a concept of governance
that is in itself organic—one that focusses on the tasks
to be undertaken and enlists, or creates, the appropri-

ate authorities, whether local, regional, provincial or even federal, to get the job done. Implementation is achieved through co-operative action among those with the necessary powers. This is how the federal government came to create Granville Island, a gem of urbanity in harmony with its local context in the heart of Vancouver. Or how the Lower Mainland Regional Planning Board (LMRPB) mapped the region's floodplain and productive agricultural lands, providing the technical basis for provincial actions to prevent floodplain settlement and create the Agricultural Land Reserve (ALR). Or how the GVRD negotiated with the province to create its sister organization, the Greater Vancouver Transportation Authority (GVTA), to implement the regional transportation and growth management plans that form (or should form) the context for provincial and federal investments in Canada's Pacific Gateway.

People are the vital ingredient in a successful matrix approach to governance of an urban region. For that reason, *City Making in Paradise* is often as much about the people behind the critical decisions as it is about the decisions themselves. Many of these people appear in different roles at different points in the book; the common threads are their vision, their long-term relationships with each other and their determination to be responsible stewards for the benefit of future generations.

Greater Vancouver is still a work in progress, and some of its major challenges are presented in the final chapter of *City Making in Paradise*. The protection of the region's livability must be supplemented by a transition to sustainability. The opportunity to provide international leadership in long-term planning for urban sustainability also lies before us, but the challenges are great. They include the need to re-establish and recommit to management of regional growth and transportation while seeing to the economic competitiveness of the region in a global context. The region's commitment to mounting the first sustainable Olympic and Paralympic Games in 2010 commands our urgent attention to the affordability of housing and the problems of homelessness, drugs and crime. At the level of fundamental social justice, it bespeaks reconciliation with the region's First Nations, whose livelihoods and culture were devastated by city building, and working together to forge a place of honour for them in their traditional territory. In the book's final chapter, two pressing questions are posed: How can we meet these challenges? What kind of leadership will help us to do so?

Pioneer Planners

THE LOWER MAINLAND
REGIONAL PLANNING BOARD

T HE LATE-SPRING SURGE of the Fraser River was
watched intensely for centuries by the people of
the Halkomelem First Nation, who installed flood-
water gauges along the river banks. Until the spring
of 1948, the worst Fraser flood known to white set-
tlers was the 1894 inundation. Lesser floods in 1921
and 1935 were described as devastating, but the dike
system of earthen bulwarks established by local farmers in the early twentieth century was mostly effective in containing the floodwaters and in calming the
annual fears of residents of the Fraser Valley at freshet
time—late May to early June. No coordinating organization had been responsible for overall dike design
and construction, however, and these defences proved
wholly inadequate for the fourth Fraser River flood in
barely fifty years.

The day-to-day weather at freshet time in 1948 was
hotter than usual, increasing the rate of liquefaction
of the "gigantic load of snow in the mountains," wrote
Bruce Hutchison in his classic study, *The Fraser*. Sudden
hot weather in B.C.'s interior intensified the snowmelt
at its sources. The dike at Agassiz gave way on May 26.
The town, strategically situated on a bend in the river,
is nearly surrounded by water, and it acts like a tap on
the Fraser's downstream flow. The breach of its dikes
not only immersed the slough that curves around the
south part of Agassiz but also caused it to overflow,
throwing the main tap open. In a matter of hours, one
third of the Lower Mainland was submerged, trigger-
ing what was until then the most destructive natural
disaster in Canadian history.

For two weeks the brown waters created a "hun-
dred-mile battlefront," according to one headline, that
covered some of the best farmland in the country. So
rich with soil and nutrients were the floodwaters that
Hutchison thought it had the look of water you could
walk on. Barns floated westward, accompanied by
drowned livestock. A swimming cat was photographed
with a mouse clinging to its back. On May 31 B.C. Premier Byron Johnson declared a state of emergency.

At its height, the 1948 Fraser River flood was a
scene reminiscent of the Normandy beaches of June 6,
1944, still fresh in the memories of many of the mil-
itary men who were at both operations. A little more

than four years after D-Day, landing craft cruised the edges of the muddy fifty-thousand-acre lake, delivering gear, food and water and taking on cattle. The frigate HMCS *Antigonish* was flagship of a task force including minesweepers that steamed farther upriver to rescue inhabitants of marooned villages. Amphibious twin-engine Canso patrol bombers taxied back and forth, searching for victims. Both railway lines in the Fraser Valley were under water. Vancouver and New Westminster were islands accessible only by air.

The Canadian navy and air force did heroic rescue work during the 1948 flood. Battle-hardened members of Princess Patricia's Light Infantry filled sandbags, and soldiers patrolled the dikes by night, looking for leaks. Even with the "First in the Field" Princess Pats hard at work, there were simply not enough personnel to do the job. The army appealed for seven hundred more volunteers. On the hottest day of the two-week ordeal, June 5, fresh troops from the prairie-based Lord Strathcona's Horse shored up the dikes surrounding Lulu Island, creating a beachhead. It was just in time: the muddy Fraser continued to rise for five more days.

"IT'S HIGHLY SIGNIFICANT that a specific event not only created the Lower Mainland Regional Planning Board (LMRPB), but made it a necessity," says Peter Oberlander. Considered by many to be the father of regional planning on the Lower Mainland, Oberlander was one of the founders of the LMRPB, the area's first regional planning agency. He also established the University of British Columbia (UBC) School of Community and Regional Planning, or SCARP.

"What was the event?" Oberlander asks, at eighty-seven still a teacher to the core. "A very important phenomenon occurred—the Fraser River flooding of '48. A monumental destructive force which destroyed farmland, houses, buildings, communities, and literally washed millions of acres of farmland down the river."

The flood was crucial in two ways, Oberlander explains. Not only did it make the case for a regional approach to planning that took all of the Lower Fraser Basin into consideration, but "we began to build dikes to regulate the river and control its flooding."

They built serious dikes. Jim Robson, for twenty-five years the voice of the Vancouver Canucks, remembers being given a day off from high school at Maple Ridge to fill sandbags in marshy Pitt Meadows and watching the dike at the east end of Barnston Island become breached by water so deep it filled his uncle's house to the upstairs level. Robson observed that the new dikes around the island were finished with a surface layer of rock from the dike to the water. The dikes around Richmond, Maple Ridge, Annacis Island and Chilliwack in particular became part of an improved network of water-control works that would stand as the Lower Mainland of B.C.'s insurance policy against flooding.

"To this day," Peter Oberlander maintains, "the diking system built after 1948 has behaved reasonably well. And since that disaster it has been clear that the river, from Hope to Delta, was a single space which had to be planned. The LMRPB was created to take on the post-disaster phase of the river and the indivisibility of its territory. The river couldn't belong to Hope; it couldn't belong to Mission. The Lower Mainland geography—ocean on the west, mountains on the north, more mountains on the east and the U.S. border—dictated a manmade, environmentally conditioned basin."

THE POLITICAL ORIGINS of the LMRPB lie in the death throes of the 1947–52 Byron Johnson coalition government, which by then was believed to be so corrupt that anyone who had lit a cigarette for a Liberal or Conservative MLA lined up for free Crown land. Tom McDonald had a more public-spirited payoff in mind. A staunch Tory, McDonald had served as both president of the B.C. Conservative Party and secretary of the B.C. division of the new Community Planning Association of Canada (CPAC). The CPAC, a creation of the federal Central Mortgage and Housing Corporation, was intended to get planning underway in Canadian cities after the war. It is entirely likely that Tom McDonald was offered rewards for organizing successful Tory leadership campaigns for Herbert Anscomb in 1946 and 1950—beating W.A.C. Bennett both times.

But McDonald was, in the estimation of both Peter Oberlander and future B.C. cabinet minister Bob Williams, "a straight arrow." His request to have a regional planning board proclaimed must have elicited snickers from those handing out the goodies.

It took a number of initiatives and coincidences to make a regional planning board possible. Harland Bartholomew and Associates, the American planners who had done the existing plan for the City of Vancouver, recommended the formation of a regional planning agency in 1946. In 1947 the B.C. Community Planning Association, CPAC's B.C. branch, with McDonald at its helm, decided to press for a regional planning board as one of its main priorities. Their reasoning was that water edges and topography were more productive to study than political boundaries. Regional planning should be planning without borders.

The massive Fraser River flood exposed the lack of any single organization responsible for flood control. Throughout 1948, discussions were held with the province about the merits of a regional planning board. That year, the provincial Town Planning Act was amended to allow the formation of regional planning areas and regional planning boards. Thus authorized, the Lower Mainland Region was confirmed as a planning area.

The Lower Mainland Regional Planning Board was created on June 21, 1949. Its first meeting was held on September 15 of that year. Tom McDonald was appointed acting secretary. Twenty-six municipalities were invited—fifteen responded, and from then on the majority of the eligible six incorporated cities, sixteen district municipalities, four villages and scattered parcels administered by the province known as Unorganized Territory were members. They covered the distance from Hope to the Gulf of Georgia and from the U.S. border to the mountains north of the Fraser, adding up to 1,600 square miles. It was agreed that municipalities could send either elected officials or staff to the meetings. An office for the LMRPB, "two bare-floored rooms" as described by the board's first executive director, Jim Wilson, was found on Columbia Street in New Westminster, and the board began official operations in September 1950. For the first time in British Columbia, an area larger than a single municipality would be seen and planned as a whole.

"We were quite conscious from the beginning," Wilson recalled in 1988, "that we would survive, even at our rock-bottom level of support, only if we proceeded pretty circumspectly. That meant tailoring our program to accord with our limited means: two research assistants, one draftsman, one secretary, myself and no unallocated cash in the budget . . . Quite a challenge."

The LMRPB was budgeted, Wilson still likes to point out, on the basis of three cents per person living in the region per year. The board wasn't able to raise

even that much. Despite the LMRPB's ambitious programs and area studies, regional planning was seen as
a political luxury.

BOB WILLIAMS HAS acquired a reputation as one of
the brightest New Democratic Party (NDP) talents of
the past thirty years in British Columbia. He started out
as a summertime gofer at Vancouver City Hall, trained
at UBC's planning school under Peter Oberlander, and
became a planner with the LMRPB in the early 1960s,
with Tom McDonald serving as secretary. Williams
was elected Vancouver alderman for a term (1966–68)
and became Minister of Everything in Dave Barrett's
1972–76 provincial government, in which capacity he
invented the Insurance Corporation of B.C. and made
the Agricultural Land Reserve a realistic notion.

Tom McDonald was Bob Williams's kind of guy,
which is to say, larger than life. "Tom was a great big
man, a giant in a way, bald, but not fashionably so. He
looked like an early Ron Basford [minister of state for
Urban Affairs in the Pierre Trudeau federal administration in the late 1960s]. He had a wonderful sonorous
voice that you could hear a block away, and yet it was
so mellifluous. He had an office in the Vancouver Block
[still a landmark on Granville Street, with its white
terra-cotta exterior finish and rooftop clock tower]. I
remember that as soon as I got out of the elevator, I
could hear his voice booming down the hall. We ended
up getting along like a house on fire. We really admired

each other. I was a young lefty and he was a wonderful, aging red Tory who talked the same language, so we were able to have a lot of fun together."

Peter Oberlander respected McDonald, too. "I owe him a lot," Oberlander says today. "He belongs in the first level of icons."

McDonald's charisma attracted loyalty and talent. His most significant hire was Jim Wilson, who had Master's degrees in Engineering from both Glasgow and MIT. Credentials or not, Wilson knew he was not emotionally an engineer, and he went on to enrol in regional planning at the University of North Carolina—"certainly one of the best planning schools of the day," in Bob Williams's opinion. Moreover, Wilson studied the Tennessee Valley Authority (TVA) during his summer vacations to see how the TVA treated the residents of the lands it had flooded during the Depression. McDonald went to the TVA looking for regional planning expertise and returned with Wilson.

"Jim was a Scottish engineer who served as the first real head of the LMRPB and managed it through all its formative years," Bob Williams recalls. By "a Scottish engineer," Williams clearly implies one of those versatile, do-anything kilted characters profiled in Arthur Herman's 2001 book, *How the Scots Invented the Modern World*. Wilson was all that and more.

Jim Wilson is a rare fusion of sheer academic brilliance—at one time, he taught at four different universities—and down-to-earth managerial savvy. It is due to his meticulousness as a report writer that we have a valuable first-hand portrait of the Lower Mainland as it existed when he arrived at the board's threadbare New Westminster office in July 1951. Much of Vancouver's infrastructure was pre–World War I in concept and design at the time, dating from the Lower Mainland boom in growth between 1907 and 1912. As Wilson recalled in 1988 in a typewritten personal memoir:

> In 1950, when the Board started its work, the settlement pattern [of the Lower Mainland] was very different from what it is today. The transportation "system" tells the story. The Lions Gate and Pattullo bridges still charged tolls; a rickety old swing bridge highly vulnerable to assaults from barge traffic stood guard over Richmond and the city-operated airport, and Ladner beyond was reached by a ferry; North Vancouver was accessible via a swing bridge where the Second Narrows stands now and a commuter ferry still ran from Vancouver to the foot of Lonsdale; Kingsway was new and uncrowded, and the old Trans-Canada Highway was in no sense a freeway, still providing direct access to abutting properties. The Lougheed Highway was still to come; the B.C. Electric Railway carried passengers between Vancouver and New Westminster and beyond.

The pattern of urban development reflected all this. Downtown Vancouver and New Westminster dominated the scene entirely; there were no modern suburban shopping centres; not a single high-rise graced the West End; the main target area for suburban development was Burnaby, growth on the North Shore, Richmond, Coquitlam and Surrey being still a dream in the minds of impatient small-holders and developers. In the Fraser Valley the small towns and settlements were clearly definable, surrounded by farms and small holdings, and the atmosphere was unmistakably rural. There were sawmills with beehive burners in [Vancouver's] False Creek; many houses still used sawdust as fuel; and "pollution" as a public problem had not yet been discovered. In short, the Lower Mainland was still at an early pre-metropolitan stage in its growth.

"WHATEVER CHANGES WERE impending," Wilson reflected, "governments in the Lower Mainland could scarcely be said to be ready in 1950." Planners, those civic early-warning radar operators, were not yet plugged in. They were beginning to trickle out of Peter Oberlander's UBC planning school, though trained, as Oberlander acknowledges today, for jobs that did not yet exist.

"The kingpin on the staff side was usually the munic-ipal clerk," Wilson recalls in his memoir, "who had prob-ably started in a lowly clerical post and had worked his way up over the years ... There were no 'planners,' or rather there was one planner-surveyor attached to the Vancouver Town Planning Commission, apart from two on the staff of the Department of Municipal Affairs in Victoria. The strongest profession as such was engineering, and the municipal engineer, if there was one, was usually the other 'power' in the hall . . .

"There was, of course, no metropolitan government—an idea guaranteed to produce shock and horror in any municipal politician. The only supra-functions, the Greater Vancouver Water District and the Vancouver and Districts Joint Sewerage and Drainage District, were devoted to the satisfaction of these obvious and compelling necessities, administered by competent, no-nonsense engineers, and seen as totally non-political."

Jim Wilson would fix all that. He and the LMRPB set their own agendas, which were written with enough savvy to get most of the board's funding from the City of Vancouver. Vancouver's council and planners saw the point of the board's central mission: managing growth. The city saw itself as almost built-out. Even before Wilson joined the board, the LMRPB's purpose was to gather data and then enter into dialogue with its member municipalities about what that information meant.

The LMRPB was made up of distinguished civic personalities whose importance has, for the most part, not lasted into the present. The executive first met informally on September 21, 1949, to make such strategic choices as the number of planners needed to do the work. The chair of the board, and of that meeting, was D.J. McGugan of New Westminster, chief engineer of the Fraser Valley Dyking Board. A key presence at the meeting was H.V. Jackson, who as early as 1936 had chaired a citizens' group called the Lower Mainland Regional Planning Association, dedicated to the idea that the Lower Mainland was a single social and economic unit and should be planned as a whole. Among the few still-recognizable names is that of R.M. Grauer of Richmond, a descendant of the pioneer Grauers; another family member was at the helm of B.C. Electric when it was purchased by W.A.C. Bennett in 1961 to become B.C. Hydro. The dominant voice at that first meeting, though, was that of Peter Oberlander, consultant to the board, who said the LMRPB's first priority must be to "document all twenty-six municipalities . . . and, in that way, establish the character of the region."

To that end, a total of $20,000 was made available for the LMRPB's activities in 1950, according to a progress report dated April 14 of that year. Central Mortgage and Housing Corporation was in for the biggest sum, $7,500. The City of Vancouver pledged $5,000. Another $2,500 came from the province. The board hoped the remaining $5,000 would be voluntarily forthcoming from the twenty-five municipalities excluding Vancouver.

The LMRPB's first major report, *The Lower Mainland Looks Ahead* (1952), was a vision of the fifty years that would end in 2002. As breathtaking as planners' projections of population growth on the Lower Mainland have been over the years, they have usually proved conservative. The LMPRB's projection was no exception. "Huge Growth Brings Issues," headlined the *Vancouver Sun* on March 1, 1952. "1.5 Million People Could 'Strangle' Lower Mainland." The message was clear enough, but, just in case, the *Sun's* editorial writer pounded home the point: "Unless we plan now, these new citizens will strangle our traffic arteries, deplete the food supply from our Fraser Valley bread-basket, pollute our bathing beaches, and create a nightmare of administrative problems."

As the LMRPB's work got underway, there wasn't always consensus over the value of planning among Lower Mainland municipalities. The board made itself useful, though, taking on tasks as utilitarian as the unified regional house-numbering system that gives Fraser Valley addresses their five-digit heft. The LMRPB did initial studies on rural and industrial land and mapped the floodplain of the Fraser River. One of the board's functions in the early days was as contract planner for the municipalities in the valley. At the same time, the small staff plugged away at an overall plan for the Lower Mainland. When *Chance and Challenge* appeared in 1964, it was one of the first overall regional planning documents in Canada.

Even as the board presented the product of fifteen years' dedicated labour, though, the signs of its demise were apparent. One sign had been the resignation of Alistair Crerar, a co-founder of the board and since its inception its assistant director. For those in the know, Crerar's departure in August 1962 may not have doomed the board, but it was a blow.

"I worked [at the LMRPB] as a summer student on the first industrial survey of the Lower Mainland," Bob Williams remembers. "Jim Wilson's second-in-command was Alistair Crerar, who was a mentor to me all of my life. I had Alistair as a deputy minister for the Environment and Land Use Secretariat when the Barrett government formed that capacity. Alistair was a wonderful character and a really great intellect. The early industrial survey in the Lower Mainland—nothing had been done that equalled it in the country, in terms of analyzing what made the region tick. And we haven't done one of those since then. That's almost fifty years ago. Alistair and Jim were great pioneers."

It was frustration that had driven Crerar from his job at the LMRPB—a frustration so intense it would eventually drive him from the planning profession. He told the press he was annoyed by the LMRPB's lack of both power and the funding to attack such issues as urban sprawl.

The LMRPB followed up *Chance and Challenge* with what is still the only overall plan for the Lower Fraser River Basin, 1966's *Official Regional Plan*. In it, the board pared the action plan arising from its 1952 report down to four recommendations. It was tiptoeing past the graveyard, living from cheque to cheque, and worried that its biggest client, the City of Vancouver, might stop paying the bills. With those realities in mind, the LMRPB neatly apportioned its requests to every level of government. It was a broad appeal for a local arm of government—one that would be unusual even today:

1. The Regional Planning Board will undertake specific studies on airports, parks and rural zoning in collaboration with other bodies, and will direct and assist local planning programs.

2. The municipalities will be asked to have a study made of the need for some form of metropolitan and valley government, and the Greater Vancouver municipalities will be asked to consider setting up metropolitan boards for planning, airports and parks.

3. The Provincial Government will be asked to prepare subdivision control legislation, undertake a land conservation program and carry out an economic survey of the region.

4. The Federal Government will be asked to set up meteorological stations, to study the need for integration of harbour authorities, and arrange for the development of Roberts Bank.

THE BOARD WAS especially prescient in calling for
the federal government to make the Roberts Bank coal
port at Tsawwassen a priority. Today, Roberts Bank is
a coal- and container-loading facility of the Vancouver Port Authority. It is located on a man-made peninsula in the Strait of Georgia, close to the Canada-U.S.
border and reached by a rail causeway parallel to the
automotive one leading to the B.C. Ferries terminal.
Although the Canadian National and Grand Trunk rail-
ways were federal Crown corporations at the time the
LMRPB report was issued, the coal completed its journey from as far away as Alberta and the U.S. to Roberts Bank on provincially controlled land. The LMRPB,
while supporting the coal port, took a stand in favour
of having the rail right-of-way include as little agricultural and recreational land as possible. W.A.C. Bennett,
who had succeeded Johnson as premier in 1952, and
who would hold the office for the next twenty years,
insisted instead on the straightest possible connection—and thereby the shortest and cheapest—from
source to tidewater's edge.

Not only did Bennett win, but he dissolved the
LMRPB in 1969 and divided the Lower Mainland
regional planning area into four regional districts, rein-
stating the mutual distrust among municipalities that
the board had striven for seventeen years to overcome.
He went even further by expropriating 8,000 hectares
of farmland adjacent to the rail right-of-way for future
industrial development. Nearly forty years later, this

land would become a component in a treaty settlement with the Tsawwassen First Nation and part of the proposed expansion of Deltaport at Roberts Bank.

The vision of the LMRPB, often attributed to Jim Wilson, had been "cities in a sea of green." The words conjured a region that, while destined for rapid growth, would always be set within a working landscape of farms, forests and protected wildlife sanctuaries. That vision led directly to the LMRPB's *A Regional Parks Plan for the Lower Mainland* in 1966, the blueprint for the magnificent system of twenty-one regional parks that exists today. Despite the board's dissolution under Bennett, the Green Zone concept articulated in the parks plan would be embedded in the *Livable Region Strategic Plan* in 1996. It would also inspire the provincial government's *Lower Mainland Nature Legacy* (1995), which would culminate in the purchase of Burns Bog, the "lungs of the Lower Mainland," in 2003.

Peter Oberlander has the long-term perspective to evaluate the record of the LMRPB. "It did three things. It produced a real plan for the whole basin. For the first time, somebody looked at it and made a land-use pattern that was a regional one. Secondly, it began the long process, and it's not complete by a long shot, of getting the municipalities to talk to each other. The City of Langley and the District of Langley are really on the same turf [for example], so quit bickering. You have a future either together or not at all. That was a very important learning process, teaching process ... So the LMRPB began to gestate the regional conscience, the regional ability, the regionality of it.

"Finally, it demonstrated the geographic, environmental context. Political boundaries are neat, tidy, and may have some administrative merit, but in reality, they are anti-planning, because they don't allow the natural environment in which we have to survive to be thought of as the whole. So the LMRPB did something specific, like the plan, and then began to introduce the geographic, environmental unit of the region and bring the municipal leaders into a continuing dialogue."

The LMRPB conducted the first detailed study of the Lower Mainland region. The board considered population growth, industrial and agricultural development, bridges, highways, airports and recreation uses, and produced the *Official Lower Mainland Regional Plan* that was adopted by twenty-eight municipalities. According to an evaluation in the City of Vancouver Archives, during its time in operation the planning board "completed 40 planning studies and compiled 850 detailed lot-by-lot development maps." It portrayed the Lower Mainland with a level of detail never seen before in Canada.

The LMRPB had also proven that an agency such as itself could deliver objective information and analysis to put the arguments over land-use decisions on a more factual basis. To those few who celebrated the loss of the LMRPB, it must have come as a disappointment when the board was replaced at the end of 1968 by the GVRD's planning department. In the following years, though, there would be hard times in store for regional planners.

BY 1966, AS Tom McDonald had intended, the Lower Mainland of B.C. had a plan for coping with growth— the first such plan in Canada. It's a plan that still looks workable today. It's easy to be preoccupied by the opportunities that were lost as the Lower Mainland subsided into parochialism. But it's more important to realize what the LMRPB's legacy is to the region we know today: a firm line between city and countryside, an outstanding system of regional parks, limited settlement in areas subject to flooding and, mundane as it might seem, a street numbering system that makes logical sense.

Saving Strathcona

THE VANCOUVER OF 1965 did not look much different from the Vancouver of the 1930s. The city had
changed the most during the first third of the twentieth century. It did not really have a skyline—just a few
taller buildings built during the city's Golden Years of
Growth (1907–12) that poked up above the others. The
Marine Building of 1929, the third Hotel Vancouver
and the Sun Tower of 1912 were the standouts against
the North Shore mountain panorama. The Hotel Vancouver had stood as an unclad, rusting steel frame
from 1928 to 1939, when it was rushed to completion
for a royal visit. City Hall was built in 1935–36. Vancouver, strictly speaking, could not afford its first purpose-
built municipal hall in the depths of the Depression, so
the building was financed entirely by debt, much of it
held by large corporations. By the mid-sixties, though,

the pent-up hunger to return to the city's Edwardian boom was palpable. Bill Rathie was elected mayor in 1962 on the slogan "Let's get Vancouver moving!"

Downtown *did* get moving soon afterward, literally. The Bentall Centre (started in 1965) and the Mac-Millan Bloedel headquarters (1968–69) were built on, then beyond, Burrard Street—a dramatic westward shift of the city's epicentre that touched off the boom Vancouver had been awaiting.

Another noteworthy shift was happening in the late sixties: Vancouver was becoming fertile ground for new ideas. From any point east of Hope, Vancouver looked to be a place where you could live a life with wider boundaries. The Flying Burrito Brothers' assertion that "Vancouver may be just my kind of town" held out hope for young American men who had got letters from their draft boards. Events of greater magnitude elsewhere were setting a template for Vancouver's status as a capital of the youth culture. In 1968 alone, Martin Luther King Jr. and Robert Kennedy were assassinated, and Pierre Trudeau was elected prime minister. Jerry Rubin, the American student activist, visited UBC in the fall of 1968 and, outrage of outrages, led a sit-in featuring a greased pig at the Faculty Club. Humankind put Neil Armstrong on the moon in July 1969. The first be-in in Stanley Park was held in 1967, and a smoke-in led to the Gastown Riot of 1971. Greenpeace was born that same summer. There was a youthful mood of experimentation, of limits to be tested. Under those conditions, the events in a single Vancouver neighbourhood would change lives not only in the city but from coast to coast.

IN THE FALL of 1968, Shirley Chan and her family were facing eviction from their comfortable house on Keefer Street in Vancouver's historic Strathcona neighbourhood. Chan, twenty-one years old at the time, attended an information meeting the night of October 17 at which the residents of the community were to learn the final outcome of the "slum-clearance" project that had been underway in Strathcona for nearly ten years. Entire blocks of charming shiplap turn-of-the-century workers' houses had been torn down to be replaced with concrete row houses and apartments. Not only was the remaining neighbourhood scheduled to be demolished for social housing, but the plan was for an elevated freeway to run down the southern blocks of the community before slashing through the southern edge of Chinatown and Gastown. The freeway would link Highway 1 with Carrall Street and continue to the Burrard Inlet waterfront and the projected 200 Granville tower, which would be constructed on a platform over the CP Rail tracks by the railway's development arm, Marathon Realty. The freeway would disgorge thousands of cars at the foot of Granville Street, and drivers would set off to the North Shore by way of either a tunnel under the harbour or a twinned Lions Gate bridge.

Most of the Strathcona residents at the meeting that night had little or no idea of the forces arrayed against them. Architect and critic Donald Gutstein had given the title *Vancouver Ltd.* to his exposé of development in a city yearning for growth. Urban renewal and freeways were all the rage in the immediate postwar climate; after defeating Hitler, Western civilization thought it could do just about anything. "Urban renewal" was the postwar expression of a North American social movement that dated back to the Edwardian era, nurturing the ambitions of pioneering city planners to provide every citizen with secure, weatherproof housing. At the same time, the continent-wide City Beautiful movement was based on the belief that inspirational urban design could uplift city dwellers, especially in cases of what it considered moral decline due to poverty. The fulfillment of these sacred objectives had been delayed by the two world wars and the Depression, and now downtown Vancouver business interests argued that the eradication of Strathcona and Chinatown was a small price to pay—no price at all, really—for the city-wide benefits the freeway promised to bestow.

Shirley Chan still remembers her first impression of Darlene Marzari, the social planner hired by the city to help Strathcona residents find new places to live. The strain was beginning to show on Marzari, who smoked cigarillos as she spoke that night and blushed, Chan thought, from acute embarrassment. There were numerous other city officials at the meeting, opposed, it seemed, only by longtime community organizer and NDP MP Margaret Mitchell and Penelope Stewart, a sympathetic UBC social work student.

Marzari was a recent graduate of the London School of Economics who had moved to Vancouver with her UBC professor husband, Frank. She explained to the meeting what she could and could not do for the 3,000 people whose houses were set to be bulldozed under Phase 3, the last and most extensive step of the plan to reduce a vibrant community to apartment blocks. Already 3,350 residents had been moved. Many of those at the meeting, especially those who spoke only Chinese dialects, had not the faintest idea why they were being turned out of their homes by the city. The notices of expropriation had been printed in English. The value of the homes in question had been frozen for years so that the city could acquire them cheaper than the market price—for about $5,000 apiece.

Marzari, sent out to reassure the neighbourhood, ended up getting an earful. The way Marzari remembers it, Shirley Chan was especially eloquent. "What you're doing is wrong," Chan told city officials. "My mom and dad put their lives into this community. They have a mortgage, they have a house. We are the children being raised in that house, and it's the same for all my friends. What you have to do is go back to the beginning and stop this whole process or at least include us in a significant way."

After the meeting Chan and Marzari went for a cup of coffee. Soon, Marzari remembers, she was agreeing that urban renewal as carried out in Strathcona was "a horrendously bad project. It was evil. We didn't realize the ramifications of what we were about to do, but I knew that something was terribly amiss. It was the best political instinct I'd ever had in my whole life."

On her way home that night, Marzari stopped in at the Cool-Aid youth social services office to find twenty-five-year-old storefront lawyer Mike Harcourt holding an open house. Something was going very wrong in Strathcona, she told Harcourt. There was a population there that had been expropriated without being heard.

"Okay," Harcourt said, "give me some names."

The next day, Marzari saw Harcourt in Strathcona talking with Shirley and Mary Lee Chan, Shirley's mother.

As Chan recalls, something else happened at the meeting with the city officials that night—something that had never happened before: "Rather than telling the residents they were unrealistic in their demands and they were too late, some of the organizers asked the residents what they wanted."

THAT YEAR, SHIRLEY Chan was a student at three-year-old Simon Fraser University (SFU), a seat of learning designed by Vancouver architect Arthur Erickson with the express purpose of inspiring its student body to question authority. If Chan is any indication, that aspect of SFU's space-age design worked as intended. Chan was uniquely qualified by upbringing, age and training to spearhead the effort to save Strathcona from those who wanted to replace the delightful hodgepodge of clapboard siding, spindle-rail front porches and intensive backyard vegetable gardens with concrete high-rise living.

Had that happened, a good deal of the city's earliest history would have been swept away. Strathcona is Vancouver's first neighbourhood. It was once the site of an Aboriginal camp, Kumkumalay, meaning "big-leaf maple trees," near the foot of Dunlevy Avenue. That was where Captain Edward Stamp built the second sawmill on Burrard Inlet in 1865. The Strathcona community was named for the Hudson's Bay executive who hammered the last spike of the Canadian Pacific Railway, Donald A. Smith, better known as Lord Strathcona. The railway managers lived in Strathcona until the beginning of the twentieth century, when most of the community's houses were built. Senior railway decision makers quickly moved on to the city's new West End.

The heart of the original Chinatown was near today's Chinese Cultural Centre and the Dr. Sun Yat-sen Garden. At that time, False Creek, a tidal inlet, flowed at high tide along low-lying Columbia Street and connected with Burrard Inlet. Starting in 1916, with the creation of Granville Island out of the dredgings of False Creek to accommodate wartime shipping, more and more of the inlet was infilled to provide new and valuable inner-city industrial sites with water access. The shrinking inlet became a toxic industrial sewer into which were dumped the effluents of mills, machine shops and wood preservatives from barrel manufacturers. Shirley Chan remembers that as late as the 1950s, buildings along the south side of Pender Street—which had once been Dupont Street, Vancouver's long-forgotten red-light district—still backed the inlet. But before long Strathcona lost its water access on the north shore of the creek from Carrall to Main streets.

Over the years, the neighbourhood had become the reception depot for subsequent waves of immigrants: Jews, Italians and Chinese. It was known during the 1930s as the East End, a derogatory name for a district that, at the time, contained near-ghettoes of Japanese and Italians separated by Hastings Street. The first inklings of a scheme to condemn the neighbourhood oozed to the surface in 1949, when a UBC study team proposed the modernization of Strathcona, calling the process "slum clearance."

During the fifties, Vancouver's city engineers repaved and relit streets, laid sewer lines, built bridges and expanded the central business district. According to the late urban geographer Walter Hardwick, successive city councils were more concerned with completing infrastructure projects than with careful planning. The new process of public involvement in planning these public works would come as "a shock to the political and bureaucratic establishment," Hardwick wrote in his 1974 book, *Vancouver.*

It may be strictly coincidence that in 1957 Strathcona became, for the first time, one-half ethnic Chinese, and a year later the *Vancouver Sun* hailed the city's urban renewal program as a much-needed cleanup of a derelict district. Strathcona was nevertheless thriving as an inner-city residential annex of Chinatown.

By 1959, erasing the late-nineteenth-century character of Strathcona was official city policy. A key objective of the City of Vancouver redevelopment study, produced that year, was the "comprehensive redevelopment" of Strathcona, which meant that two thirds of the neighbourhood would be rebuilt as social housing, townhouses and apartment buildings. Some of the newly constructed complexes would be built on existing parklands, making necessary the destruction of yet more houses to replace the green space. Everything south of Prior Street would be levelled to make room for the elevated six-lane freeway.

Despite the city's freeze on property assessments and a ban on home improvements, both imposed in 1958, Strathcona residents "made strenuous efforts to maintain the comfort and appearance of their homes," a City Hall report acknowledged. But once condemned, the neighbourhood didn't linger long. Heavy equipment rumbled into Strathcona in 1959, flattening a block of homes adjacent to MacLean Park and taking down the houses on ten more acres. In 1960 the Chinese Benevolent Association (CBA) cried foul, urging that the residents of Strathcona be allowed to rebuild their neighbourhood themselves. Nonetheless, between 1961 and 1967, under Phase 1 of the plan, 1,600 people were out of house and home, and twenty-eight acres of land were cleared. The second phase, which began in 1965, displaced 1,730 people from twenty-nine acres of cleared land. In 1968, when city council asked for federal approval to implement the final stages of demolition, Phase 3, it was seen as a routine request. Donald Gutstein has written that city council's ulterior motive for Phase 3 was to divert newly available federal funding from urban renewal to the proposed freeway.

BOB WILLIAMS, VANCOUVER city alderman from 1964 to 1966, was in a good position to understand the larger forces at work in the Strathcona urban renewal program and freeway proposal. Among the members of that council, he alone objected to the scheme. As Williams recalls,

> The planning department in Vancouver was all Englishmen in those days. No Canadians need apply. Gerald Sutton-Brown was a classic colonial type,

and he became city manager. After high school I
ended up working at City Hall as a clerk, and then
a draftsman in the Engineering Department. I
went on to UBC in economics, geography and planning. But there was no way that I would ever have
been employed in the Vancouver City Planning
Department.

Sutton-Brown's office, when he was the first
planner, was on the tenth floor of the building. I
was the kid who read the rain gauge every morning
on the roof. So I would go up through the planning
department, up to the attic and onto the roof. When
I came back, the other draftsmen would be tucking
their handkerchiefs up their sleeves à la English
elite, and they would say to me, "Back, are you? How
are things in the foreign office?" That was the way it
was in those days. It was scandalous. Those bloody
Limeys ended up doing the urban renewal stuff.
And they were totally insensitive, totally arrogant
bastards. Totally insensitive "slum clearance" non-
sense. All the worst in planning in North America
came with those bastards.

Their plan was to wipe out Strathcona—there
was federal money available. After I was elected as
an alderman, I would raise it in city council with
Sutton-Brown, who was by then the city manager,
and I said, "You know and I know the process: you
do a windshield survey of that neighbourhood. One
of you bloody Englishmen drives down in your car

and says yes, no, bad, good, da da da, and then you make some decisions about moving a bulldozer in."

I ended up meeting some of the Chinese Canadians in Strathcona, and it shocked the hell out of me. In those days, their houses were cheap as borscht. These were poor people. The city would offer them the [so-called] market price, but there was nowhere else in the city where you could buy a house for that money.

I got up at city council and challenged Sutton-Brown and the mayor, Bill Rathie, and said, "This is madness. Do you know what you're doing? You're destroying the lives of these people. They'll never be able to own another house. Their whole sense of being, their livelihood is shot."

MAYOR TOM CAMPBELL, elected in November 1967 along with a Non-Partisan Association city council majority, continued to promote Rathie and Sutton-Brown's agenda, which had the support of the most influential people in the city. The business elite looking to revive downtown Vancouver was spurred on further after being reminded by prodigal son Pierre Berton (writing in the *Toronto Star*, no less) that the southwest corner of the strategic Georgia and Granville intersection, site of the second Hotel Vancouver until it was demolished in 1949, had been a parking lot far too long for a first-class city to tolerate. The new freeway was seen as part of the solution to the downtown core's stagnation. Its supporters argued that the freeway would enrich the retail life there by moving traffic in huge numbers from the eastern suburbs to the foot of Granville Street and back. Along with a third crossing of Burrard Inlet, a new freeway would also encourage property development on the North Shore.

The late Woodrow Wilson "Bud" Wood, among many others, didn't think the freeway was such a hot idea, though. As opposition to the proposal built, Wood became fond of demonstrating what the effect of the east-west freeway would be on the little Chinatown building—the World's Thinnest Building, at that—on the second floor of which Wood and his partner, Bill Birmingham, ran their small, principled architectural firm, Birmingham & Wood. Their office, which now houses Jack Chow Insurance, was directly across Pender Street from the building in which Dr. Sun Yat-sen, the father of Chinese democracy, hid out from the agents of the dowager empress during his fundraising tour in 1911.

Many times, with journalists and others, the lanky Wood stood out on Pender Street, at the southwest corner of the intersection with Carrall Street, and pointed out that the freeway's westbound ramp to Seymour Street would put a thirty-foot-high, two-hundred-foot-wide structure on an intersection fifty feet wide, its thousands of tonnes of reinforced concrete looming within one foot of the building's easternmost window.

Bud Wood was not only a practising architect; he also taught design at the UBC School of Architecture, where he held workshops to draw up urban designs for sites likely to come into play in the city. He had a mob of idealists in his classes—student architects who were appalled at what city councillors, planners, engineers, the city planning commission and even some famous architects were proposing with the freeway.

"Arthur Erickson," Wood would fulminate, "actually proposes to humanize this whole abortion by designing Moon Gates"—circular openings used in Chinese architecture to frame views into, say, garden courtyards— "along the retaining walls of the ramp to give it a flavour of Chinatown, even as the freeway destroys it."

The day after Wood found out about the freeway ramp, dozens of student architects demonstrated against the river of concrete.

SHIRLEY CHAN'S PARENTS had instilled in her an appetite for community activism. Her mother, Mary Lee Chan, worked long hours in the rag trade for such Water Street outfits as the Atlas Leather company. Mrs. Chan would arrive home after a hard day's work, help make dinner, pick up a shopping bag full of flyers, "and then we'd go out together door-knocking and asking people to sign a petition," Shirley Chan remembers.

"My dad, Walter Chan, used to write articles for the *Chinese Times* to get the community to come out, to stand up for their rights, to have a say, to join SPOTA, the Strathcona Property Owners and Tenants Association. Although he was a non-smoker and non-drinker, he was sick with liver disease. My mom being the legs, my dad being the writer, he worked for the Chan Family Association as well as for our family store, the Kuo Sen International dry goods store at East Pender and Columbia streets. He was articulate, scholarly and highly respected."

Shirley Chan's family was offered $6,000—more than many—for their house, but that was much less than an equivalent house in another neighbourhood would have cost. Mike Harcourt recalls today,

> Shirley and Darlene Marzari came to see me. They wanted me to come to this community meeting at the Gibbs Boys Club. [The building was itself a historic site in Strathcona, being the former Schara Tzedeck synagogue, built in 1921 for an earlier wave of immigration into the neighbourhood. It is now condominiums.]
>
> There was about 70 per cent spoken in Chinese and 30 per cent in English. I sort of didn't get the flow of it. It was a long, long meeting. At the end of it, Shirley and Darlene said to me, "Well, you've been hired."
>
> "Okay. To do what?"
>
> "To stop the freeway."
>
> "Who are we taking on?"

They said, "Don't worry about it. We're just taking on the city, the province, the federal government, the development industry, the transportation and car industries, the oil and gas industry. Other than that, don't worry about it."

We all agreed that was not the kind of city we wanted: an elevated freeway all the way from Stanley Park, all the way through the downtown, wiping out Gastown, Chinatown and most of the east-side neighbourhoods, with high-rises to warehouse poor people in. Instant slums. I thought, "This doesn't seem like a very good idea to *me*."

THE PROBLEM WITH urban renewal was as much in how it was administered—top down and in secret—as in the schemes themselves. In late 1968, newly elected reform aldermen Art Phillips and Walter Hardwick were reduced to conducting title searches to figure out which houses the city was secretly buying in Strathcona. Hardwick went on to condemn contemporary planning practices in his seminal book *Vancouver*.

"The [urban] renewal policies were based upon a view of the neighbourhood that utilized physical planning criteria; in no way was the resident population consulted," he wrote. "In fact, the planners wrote in their report that the people would all be happy to be given new, clean accommodation. It was assumed that no one in his right mind would oppose urban renewal..."

Nor did the proposed freeway and further urban renewal of Strathcona seem like such a terrific idea to the federal minister responsible for housing, Paul Hellyer. Ottawa knew there were problems with a "slum-clearance" program underway in Toronto's Annex as well as with the program in Strathcona. Here was a possible opportunity for the feds to save money budgeted for demolitions and new construction. After more than three hundred elderly Chinese showed up on the steps of Vancouver's City Hall to protest the city's plan, Hellyer came west with his federal Task Force on Housing and Urban Development staff, which included a young and open-minded executive assistant named Lloyd Axworthy. At a public meeting held on November 7, 1968, they listened as Shirley Chan explained the plight of the Chinese families being turfed out of their homes.

"The urban renewal scheme is a ten-year-old plan," Chan told the task force. "It was initiated in 1957. Urban renewal has been proven to be psychologically bad, yet you are going through with it. Your aim is to give fair market value for a home, but is it fair? How do you judge the 'value to owner' when the home is in an area I have grown up in? The median price given for homes is $7,000–8,000. The displaced homeowner does not get a lump sum payment; rather, the total is calculated into 'monthly rent.' The monthly rent is used up during the waiting period—waiting to get

into public housing. You are tearing the Chinese community apart. There are 789 families living in the area
now. Most people have paid off a thirty-year mortgage,
and now they must pay off another thirty-year loan.
My parents are too old to get another mortgage, and
where are they going to live if they lose this house?
There is a shortage of housing, and yet you are going
to tear down livable homes. What right will we have to
come back into the area?"

On the following morning, November 8, Chan and
Darlene Marzari gave the federal visitors a tour of Chinatown and Strathcona. It was brave of Marzari, a new
employee at City Hall, to have dreamed up this tour
at a bar the night before, and to return from it with
Paul Hellyer in the task force's two-car motorcade to
a fifty-person audience of curious city staff. Among
them was Maurice Egan, Vancouver's director of social
planning, who had hired Marzari and was fully aware
that his job, not to mention Marzari's, was on the line.
Egan remembers the collective murmur that Marzari's
emergence from one of the cars elicited.

Egan got the call from upstairs later that morning: he was summoned to a meeting of the department
heads in Sutton-Brown's penthouse office. Not one of
his colleagues stood up for Egan. "Everybody wilted,"
Egan remembers. Not everyone in the city manager's
office was aware, though, that as a former alderman on
Ottawa city councils headed by the acerbic Charlotte

Whitton, Egan knew a thing or two about political survival. He was on the line to his contacts in Ottawa that
night, outflanking Sutton-Brown and assessing the
climate around urban renewal there. He would easily
outlast his boss. As for Chan and Marzari, the two
young women were so closely in tune with Hellyer's
viewpoint that they helped draft the telegram from
Vancouver, signed by the housing minister, that froze
urban renewal funding across Canada.

The City of Vancouver was dragged kicking its feet
towards the solution that had been obvious all along.
As early as 1960, the Chinese Benevolent Association
(CBA) had suggested using the eleven-million-dollar
demolition fund to underwrite thousand-dollar house
renovations in Strathcona. The neighbourhood could
serve as a prototype in an experimental program to
fix up old houses instead of bulldozing them. Both the
province and Ottawa, who between them had contributed 80 per cent of the costs of urban renewal, were
committed to residential rehabilitation by 1969. The
federal government had the means to carry out the
CBA's request through their Central Mortgage and
Housing Corporation; it simply required a change of
policy. The Strathcona Property Owners and Tenants
Association, the neighbourhood organization formed
in December 1968, repeated the request for Strathcona to pioneer the residential rehabilitation program,
which would be the first of its kind in Canada.

Paul Hellyer had quickly grasped the logic of rehabilitation rather than bulldozer renewal. It would
save his cash-strapped agency millions. His successor,
Robert Andras, travelled the 2,500 miles west from
Ottawa in August 1969 to hammer the point across to
a Vancouver city council who, in response, trotted out
the same dog-eared reports urging the demolition of
Strathcona. When city council finally caved that September, Andras declared that no federal money would
be available for a rehabilitation program unless residents were among its directors. Members of SPOTA
began meeting as equals with representatives of all
three levels of government, the first-ever such neighbourhood group to do so.

MIKE HARCOURT HAD acted as the pro bono legal
adviser to the Strathcona Property Owners and Tenants Association since its formation. He had first provided legal counselling to Chinese seniors who were
considering standing in front of bulldozers or climb-
ing aboard the buses headed for City Hall. Protest did
not come easily to these people. They had every reason
to be upset, from the five-hundred-dollar head tax
imposed by the Canadian government in 1903 to the
outright exclusion of Chinese immigrants that produced a lost generation of married but single men in
Vancouver separated from their wives in China until
1947 (when full citizenship was extended to them and

all other eligible Chinese). Yet the Chinese in Vancouver had not demonstrated since the Anti-Asiatic Riots of 1907, when they were provoked beyond their characteristic restraint. Harcourt, barely out of law school in 1968, advised SPOTA and the Chinatown Merchants Association on their tactics with the press and the three levels of government. He also advised the Strathcona residents who negotiated the agreement to use the federal funds intended for Phase 3 demolitions to underwrite a pilot project that would finance home and neighbourhood upgrades.

The freeway proposal was a different matter. It had been an issue longer than urban renewal, and although there was widespread opposition to it, there was impressive support. "The development industry, downtown business interests, growth-oriented city officials and aldermen and . . . Sutton-Brown all agreed that further development of downtown depended on new freeway access," notes John Punter in *The Vancouver Achievement,* his admirable history of planning and development in Vancouver from that time to the present.

Although the damage the freeway would cause was not limited to one community, it would erase much of Chinatown. The plan was "the latest abuse in eighty-one years of racial injustice and discrimination against Vancouver's Chinese," said Foon Sien Wong, head of the CBA, in late 1967. "They are not simply interfering with Chinatown. They are sticking a concrete knife into its heart. The city officials cannot, or will not, understand that they are not just dealing with streets and buildings. They are dealing in human lives, in a unique ethnic community, too fragile to survive a policy that puts pavement ahead of people."

Public pressure against the freeway had been mounting throughout 1967. The 1,300 irate citizens who jammed two volatile meetings at City Hall in November and December of 1967 made no bones about their anger towards city politicians, especially Mayor Tom Campbell, because of the lack of public consultation. Peter Oberlander, then chairman of the city-appointed planning commission, read the commission's endorsement of the freeway proposal despite his personal opposition to it, then announced his resignation and got a standing ovation from the 800 attendees led by Walter Hardwick.

In January 1968, city council scrapped plans for the crosstown freeway while approving two components, the Georgia and Dunsmuir viaducts, for construction. (The Third Crossing element of the proposal continues to have a life of its own. In tunnel form, a third crossing of Burrard Inlet as proposed by Arthur Erickson in 1990 would bypass downtown Vancouver entirely, surfacing near the B.C. Hydro substation on Main Street.)

The freeway debate, Narissa Chadwick argues in her Master's thesis, *Regional Planning in British Columbia*, was "a key issue encouraging public interest and participation in urban and regional planning." In fact, it galvanized public opinion on a planning issue for the first time in Vancouver.

"Certainly the freeway debate was absolutely strategic, central and probably historic in shaping the Vancouver we have today," Peter Oberlander says today. "No question about it. Mike Harcourt and I were on the same barricades and have the scars to prove it."

Toronto, too, would escape the worst of freeway mania when the Ontario governmnet cancelled its north-south thoroughfare, the Spadina Expressway, in 1971. Jane Jacobs, the outstanding urbanist, had moved to Toronto in 1969, on the heels of a successful fight she and others had waged against the Lower Manhattan Freeway, which would have flattened parts of New York's Greenwich Village and SoHo. Jacobs and Toronto civic activists such as John Sewell and David Crombie shared their expertise with Chan, Marzari and Harcourt as the revitalization of Strathcona got underway.

In 1972 The Electors Action Movement (TEAM) was elected to a landslide majority of Vancouver city council seats, two of which were occupied by Mike Harcourt and Darlene Marzari. Former alderman Art Phillips became mayor on a platform that included the advocacy of a rapid transit system for Vancouver. Phillips, in one of his first acts as mayor-elect, fired Gerald Sutton-Brown.

Once Strathcona had been saved, neighbouring Chinatown became easier to rescue. It could not have survived without a vibrant residential community nearby. More than that, Vancouver began softening the hard distinction between downtown and bedroom suburbs, a process still underway today: Art Phillips used to call downtown living "living over the shop." The freeway fight gave Vancouver the distinction of being the largest city in North America without a freeway clogging its arteries.

As Marzari sums it up today, "Strathcona was the first community that stood up and said, 'You can't do this to my neighbourhood.' "

MIKE HARCOURT BECAME mayor of Vancouver in 1981, serving six years in that position. During his years as B.C.'s premier from 1991–96, he would oversee a rebirth of regional planning, which had been decimated during the Social Credit cutbacks of the early '80s. Darlene Marzari did the political grunt work on that project, serving for several years as the NDP's minister of Municipal Affairs. Shirley Chan also continued in public service, working for Indian and Northern Affairs Canada before accepting a position as Mayor Mike Harcourt's executive assistant. Since then she has served on the UBC Board of Governors, including two terms as chair, and is currently a regional director general with Health Canada.

"It does not happen often in life," Mike Harcourt writes in his memoir *A Measure of Defiance*, "but Darlene Marzari and Shirley Chan are two people whom you can point to and say, 'They are *the* reason why Vancouver is as attractive a city as it is today. These two women truly helped save our city. The Strathcona Property Owners and Tenants Association is the single most significant reason why Vancouver is such a profoundly livable city today."

THREE

The Agricultural
Land Reserve

BOB HOPE ONCE said that making money in real estate is easy. All you have to do is go to the edge of town and buy the land. The results are anything but funny, though. The loss of farmland to urban sprawl leads to isolated subdivisions, strip malls and multi-storey fast-food signs—the all-too-familiar tableaux of fertile agricultural land covered over with vast parking lots and cul-de-sacs. No wonder B.C.'s New Democratic government wanted to put a stop to it.

In 1971–72, Sigurd Peterson was a man with a plan. The bureaucrat was looking for someone in power to take his draft blueprint for protecting farmland and ground-test it. Soon after Dave Barrett's NDP won the provincial election on August 30, 1972, the person in power Peterson found was Dave Stupich, the NDP member of the legislature for Nanaimo. Nanaimo had a fairly typical mid-sized city's asphalt precinct of car dealers, fast-food franchises and malls stretching north from town. Stupich was looking for a plan to limit sprawl.

By mid-September of that year, Stupich and Peterson were, respectively, provincial minister and deputy minister of Agriculture. From the moment each saw in the other what he needed, the road to the Agricultural Land Reserve (ALR) was paved with the best of intentions. Armed with Peterson's plan, Stupich set out to fulfill the dream legacy of a social democrat's political career. Back in 1950, the Co-operative Commonwealth Federation, or CCF (the NDP's predecessor), had endorsed the idea of combating the ongoing loss of prime farmland by buying the land, banking it, and encouraging farmers to keep it in production. The Lower Mainland Regional Planning Board agreed. Its 1952 report, *The Lower Mainland Looks Ahead*, stated "We will someday have to supply more than twice our present population with fresh milk, fresh fruit and vegetables. It is utter folly to sacrifice our most fertile land on the altar of unproductive residential use when more suitable land is available."

Ten years later, in a 1962 report entitled *Land for Farming*, the LMRPB drew attention to the region's agricultural land-loss problem. Its comprehensive plan *Chance and Challenge*, released in 1964, designated more than half the usable land in the Lower Fraser Valley for long-term agricultural use.

Prior to becoming a deputy minister, Sigurd Peterson had been production services director for the B.C.
Department of Agriculture. Like many others in the
department, he was concerned about the loss of farmland in the Fraser Valley. Despite the LMRPB's recommendations, the best agricultural land in B.C. was
being developed for non-agricultural uses at a faster
and faster rate. Peterson wrote an extensive report
dated December 1971 that urged the Social Credit
government to freeze sales of farmland while the
value of each parcel was assessed for what the report
called "farm use value" and "non-farm use value." The
difference between those figures, Peterson proposed,
would be a parcel's "developmental value," the amount
of which would determine whether the government
might buy the parcel on the real estate market and
then bank or lease it.

All three opposition parties made similar proposals part of their election platforms the next August.
The NDP's platform, *Policies for People,* promised "a land
zoning program to set aside areas for agricultural production" and "a land bank to purchase existing and
rezoned agricultural land for lease to farmers on a
long-term basis." One of the people who'd helped draft
an earlier NDP resolution in favour of a land act, in
1964–65, was Harold Steves, who had entered politics
expressly for that purpose. Steves had returned home
from agricultural college in the late 1950s to learn that

three-quarters of his father's land had been rezoned by Richmond city council as residential property. Harold's father was denied a permit to build the barn that would have enabled him to keep his milk quota; that was the city's way of informing him that most of his farm had been rezoned. Harold Sr. switched to cattle, only to be hit with residential property taxes. He was forced to sell most of a 130-year-old family holding. Steves would remain active on the issue throughout a political career that included a total of thirty-four years on Richmond city council and a term as an MLA in the NDP government headed by Dave Barrett.

Prior to the 1972 election, at least two members of the Social Credit majority in the legislative assembly, Delta MLA Bob Wenman and Minister of Agriculture Cyril Shelford, had wanted to see farmland preservation added to the government's program. Shelford thought enough of Sigurd Peterson's proposal that he had presented it to cabinet, only to have Premier W.A.C. Bennett dismiss it as "too politically hot." Bennett was willing to put $25 million—pocket change—into greenbelt acquisition and let it go at that.

With the NDP in power, everything changed. Dave Stupich had grown up on the prairies, that Big Sky hothouse of new ideas, and his goal with the Agricultural Land Reserve was nothing less than to take back, property by property, the good earth that is the birthright of us all.

British Columbia's agricultural capacity is minuscule for a province consisting of a million-square-kilometre land mass, three times as big as that of France. Only 5 per cent of B.C.'s land is arable, and of that less than 1 per cent is rated Class One for its ability to support intensive cultivation of "the very widest range of vegetables, cereal grains, forages, berry fruits and numerous specialty crops," as the B.C. Land Commission would characterize the most fecund of the farmland it was created to protect.

In his 1985 research paper "Sausage Making in British Columbia: The Creation of the Land Commission Act, August 1972–April 1973," Andrew Petter sums up the Barrett government's increasingly urgent problem regarding land: "While losses of agricultural land during the 20 years preceding 1971 were offset by gains achieved through new clearing, the gains were achieved in low-yield grazing areas in the north and the interior, whereas the losses occurred in the fertile valley bottoms, the coastal plains and the river basins adjacent to the province's urban centres—areas whose soil and climate made them 'best suited to intensive cultivation.' By 1973 an estimated 20 per cent of all arable land in the Lower Fraser Valley—the most productive land in the province—had been lost to residential and urban development, and a further 3,000 acres were being eaten away each year."

New subdivisions at the edges of Kamloops, Penticton, Greater Vancouver and Victoria were likely to be built on prime agricultural land unless that land was protected. The need for a public voice in determining the use of such a precious resource was more critical in B.C. than almost anywhere else in North America.

In no time flat, Stupich was ready with legislation. To hear the likes of Frank Richter tell it, the future of Western civilization itself was at stake in late February 1973, when Dave Barrett's five-month-old government tabled Bill 42, the Land Commission Act. The introduction of the bill was preceded by a freeze on sales of farmland to halt eleventh-hour speculation. Richter, opposition leader in the B.C. legislature while W.A.C. Bennett enjoyed a world cruise, sent a telegram directly to Prime Minister Pierre Trudeau, urging him to intervene. "Bill 42 ... is ... an unprecedented example of ... denying in every respect the principles in the Canadian Bill of Rights," Richter sputtered. "The Bill of Rights is of such importance to the sanctity of our Canadian way of life ... [Bill 42 is] a total contravention of the Canadian Bill of Rights and the British North America Act.

"We appeal to you as prime minister of Canada in shocked disbelief that a Canadian legislature could consider such a statute."

The doomsday rhetoric was picked up by other opposition politicians. Social Credit farm critic Don Phillips claimed in an interview with the *Province* newspaper that the Land Commission Act was "one of the most vicious pieces of legislation I've ever seen, and I could hardly believe I could witness the tabling of such legislation in a free country... [It] gives complete dictatorial powers to take land from anybody without compensation."

W.A.C. Bennett rushed back to Victoria, debarking his cruise at Buenos Aires to denounce the Land Act as "worse than anything in South America." He would confront Bill 42's "Communist" threat to all we hold dear, he vowed. He called Barrett a "Marxist."

"What kind?" was Barrett's retort. "Harpo? Zeppo? Groucho?"

"Stay calm," Barrett advised his opponents. "Read the bill."

"The hysteria they attempted to create was effective in the beginning," Dave Barrett says today, "but as the debate marched on and the newspapers began to reflect on some of their own hysterical editorials... the emotions cooled down a bit. The ridiculous behaviour of some people who should have known better didn't get mitigated until the general population got ahead of the politicians and began to understand: There's a basis for [the Land Commission Act]. There's reason and logic for it. The support is not confined to political ideologues of either the left or the right."

The critics were so shrill at the time, though, that they made Bill Vander Zalm by comparison the quiet voice of reason. Vander Zalm, then mayor of Surrey, thought some kind of agricultural land protection was "necessary."

Barrett was a cool customer, but his own words were nowhere nearly as effective as a telegram he read aloud in the legislature. It said:

"Dear Mr. Premier,

"I thoroughly support enactment of the Land Act, and can see no real validity in objections which deal with detailed provisions necessary for efficient operations. [The] act reasonably administered [is] most important to all our people. As counsel for British Columbia Fruit Growers Association and Marketing Organization in the Okanagan for over 15 years, I remember that year after year growers urged legislation to stop loss of agricultural land to developers.

"As to the Lower Fraser Valley in 1955, the Clyne Commission report on milk marketing, pages 15 and following, warned of serious dangers of subdivision of land in municipalities of Richmond, Delta, Surrey, and in the Lower Fraser Valley generally."

Barrett waited, savouring the moment, before reading the last sentence of the telegram: "You may use this telegram as you see fit in support of legislation covered by Bill 42.

"Signed, the Hon. T.G. Norris."

The same Thomas G. Norris who had beaten W.A.C. Bennett for the leadership of the B.C. Conservative Party in 1937? The Hon. Justice T.G. Norris of the B.C. Court of Appeal?

"This is a guy who was conservative, a highly respected jurist, certainly not a member of the NDP—

if anything, probably a strong Conservative Party supporter," Barrett recalls. "Now, this was a wind-sucker—
it took the wind out of their sails. There were rational
people, responsible citizens of this province who came
out during the debates supporting the legislation."

The situation was clearly urgent at the time Bill 42
was conceived. But as at least one member of the NDP
cabinet realized, the proposed land act had a number
of flaws. One of them was Stupich and Peterson's fail-
ure to provide a realistic estimate of the costs. Or, in
fact, to provide any worthwhile budget or startup figures at all.

In his eagerness to promote a farmland preservation bill, Dave Stupich had short-circuited the new
cabinet by speaking directly to farmers and developers.
He was looking to move farmland preservation up the
list of government priorities and slip it through the
legislature with hardly anyone noticing.

Andrew Petter's 1985 research paper confirms that
this was Stupich's plan. "There appears to be only one
explanation," Petter writes, "which can account for
all of Stupich's actions—an explanation to which he
himself has alluded [to me]. It is that he was so bent
on implementing his (i.e., Peterson's) program with
or without approval, regardless of the cost, that he
decided to lock the cabinet into a public commitment
without first consulting it."

"The guy was one of the most highly principled individuals I have ever met," Dave Barrett says of Stupich

today. "One of the kindest, most open-handed people. There was no guile. He gave a whole handshake. He was highly respected in his community... Stupich was a practising Christian who had deep convictions about what he was doing as a social democrat. The only fault with him in public life was that he was an ingenue— he believed everything. No survival instinct, no rough edge, no aggressiveness. What he said, he meant. He was always calm. Even in the debates he was a gracious person."

Bob Williams, by now a member of Barrett's cabinet, was in a better position than most to estimate those costs. He had been with the LMRPB in 1963 when the board designated more than half the Fraser Valley's acreage as farmland. As a Vancouver alderman from 1964–66, and then as MLA for Vancouver East, he understood the issues very well. Williams was already carrying a heavy load in the legislature. As minister of Lands, Forests, Water Resources, Recreation and Conservation, he was juggling the equivalent of three portfolios. When he took on rewriting the Peterson-Stupich legislation, he had no idea what a marathon he was facing. As Willams recalls now,

Essentially, this had been a statute that the Ministry of Agriculture had had on the shelf forever, waiting for a naive government to come along and implement it. Most ministries are like that if they're doing their work. As my friend Alistair Crerar used to say, "A good civil servant is waiting for the window of opportunity," and he has his bags packed, in terms of statutes or whatever, and he grabs the bag and runs for the window when the opportunity comes along. And Dave Stupich was that kind of naive opportunity.

They [the Department of Agriculture] hadn't carried out any real analysis, in terms of a lot of the implications. I was lucky that I had this planning background, and I had Norman Pearson [another former LMRPB staffer] with me as an assistant. I got Norman to do some work, particularly around the question of compensation [for farmers], because that is something that I had studied, in particular what the Brits did for compensation for designation and zoning. The tradition in the British system is that you don't compensate. It is simply the right of the Crown to do these things. That was the view I held, and that was the big fight in cabinet. Do we pay all these farmers off for the ALR designation? And I said, "Not a chance, not a bloody chance!" Stupich had just accepted the ministry stuff, so when Norman and others carried out an analysis, [they found that Bill 42] would have broken the bank in terms of compensating everybody. My counterargument was, "Stupich, if you want to bring in other legislation to help the farmers, do it, but do it independently of this. If you want crop insurance or a pension plan for farmers, do it, but it ain't gonna be here and it isn't going to be on our backs in terms of paying a king's ransom for the zoning, the ALR designation."

THE FIGURE PEARSON came up with for the Land Commission's startup years, with compensation, totalled $3 billion.

"I readily won that battle once they understood what the numbers were," Bob Williams says. "By then, it was so chaotic, Stupich really wasn't on top of it. The whole thing got quietly shifted over to my office. I brought in [municipal lawyer] Bill Lane to handle the actual drafting of the legislation. We put him in a side office near my ministerial office and went at it through that whole period. We ended up with fourteen drafts or something."

Bill Lane was a lawyer who had dreamed of being an architect. He might have settled for being a city planner but found a way to specialize in municipal law, working at the zoning end of development rather than on the urban design side. In time, he had become the City of Richmond's chief counsel.

"Bill was a lovely, lovely guy," Williams says today, "sharp as hell, and he had done wonderful work in Richmond in terms of preserving the dikes and the shoreline areas, in a similar kind of designation capacity. Richmond had some of the best planning in the region, between Bob McMath, a great city councillor who chaired the LMRPB for a long time, and Bill Lane.

In fact, Bill taught planning law at UBC almost until his death."

Peter Oberlander also admired Lane's civic commitment. "He was a brilliant lawyer who saw himself as a lawyer making the difference in planning—very rare. When he had a choice, he chose the public domain, both as the first municipal lawyer for Richmond and as someone who drafted, crafted and wrote creative bylaws, not for the development community, but for the community of you and me. He was the most significant mind in this field. He chose to apply his talents in the area of public policy, to try to make the municipal provincial system work. He was the first municipal-lawyer in the province, full-time."

Getting Lane to draft and then administer the Land Commission Act was Williams's master stroke. The resulting commission was born in discord, but it was soon untouchable. Not that Williams got everything he wanted out of the exercise.

"The intent when we were playing with it conceptually was that the act might be even more comprehensive than it ended up. So that [it would have been] possible for us to end up defining greenbelt areas and even toy with the idea of the Crown replacing buyers in greenbelt areas [for a short interval] where we were anxious to get some river preservation or whatever. At the end, as the fiery crosses moved across the province over the whole idea of the Land Commission, these additional wrinkles that appealed to me became impossible."

The Land Commission issued its first report, *Keeping the Options Open*, in 1975. "The Land Commission has been described as the coordinator of activity at the boundaries where town and country meet," the report said. "The commission also believes that one of the most effective ways of protecting the farming community is by helping cities solve problems which in the past were handled by the naïve expedient of encroaching more and more upon the countryside.

"An Agricultural Land Reserve is best described as a form of zoning that protects the land from the encroachment of non-agricultural development and limits the use of land within the reserve to agricultural and other uses that do not diminish the capability of the land to produce crops."

FOR A STATUTE conceived in such an uproar, the Land Commission Act and the Agricultural Land Reserve have lived long and useful lives. Because the most fertile farmland in B.C. is located close to the province's urban concentrations, fresh produce is easily available at farmers' markets. Abbotsford and Barnston Island in the Lower Fraser River have had proposed exclusions from the ALR intensely scrutinized. Even when there is a history of consistent removals from the ALR, as there has been around Chilliwack during the past five years, the land act process brings the exclusions to public attention.

The most notorious ALR exclusion process, for part of the Spetifore Lands on the Lower Mainland's Boundary Bay, lasted fifteen years. It resulted in the exclusion of productive lands from the land reserve, in a planning stalemate that has prevented the development of those lands to this day and in the elimination of the planning responsibilities of regional districts.

Much of the Spetifore Lands were never designated as farmland. The soil has had its nutrients leeched out by salt water from adjacent Boundary Bay to the point where the land is barely usable for grazing. George Spetifore applied to develop housing on the part of his land left undesignated by the original land commission surveys soon after the Land Commission Act was passed in 1973. The GVRD intervened, concerned that the last opportunity to enlarge Boundary Bay Regional Park was slipping through its fingers.

In 1979 the chair of the GVRD Park Committee, Coquitlam Mayor Jim Tonn, arranged to have the municipality of Delta sponsor a deal whereby it would ask the provincial cabinet to remove the designated Spetifore Lands from the ALR in return for turning some of the acreage over to the GVRD for the park. The province signalled that it would be prepared to authorize the exclusion. As compelling as these events might seem, there was a problem: in order to permit urban development, Delta would have to amend its community plan, which in turn would require an amendment to the GVRD's Official Regional Plan. Gerard Farry, GVRD director of planning, was determined that he and his staff should assess the proposed amendment on its own merits, rather than having its outcome driven by the benefits of additional parkland. "Gerard showed a lot of courage and integrity in standing up for the planning process and in resisting Tonn and the others who were in such haste to grease the skids for the deal," Ken Cameron says today.

The planning staff's analysis found that creating additional housing so far from jobs and services was contrary to planning policies, and Farry recommended against the amendment. The GVRD board overruled the staff recommendation, however, and gave first, second and third reading to the necessary amending bylaw in the fall of 1979. All that remained was a fourth reading for final adoption, usually a formality that was postponed until the province had considered the ALR exclusion request. But 1979 was a municipal election year, and a change in the representation from the City of Vancouver on the GVRD board included the appointment of newly elected mayor Mike Harcourt. The province took more than a year to approve the exclusion request, during which time the GVRD updated its Official Regional Plan; that meant a new bylaw would be needed to implement the Spetifore exclusion. When the GVRD board considered the matter on March 25, 1982, the directors were evenly split—twelve for and twelve against. When the decision was put to a vote in the GVRD's system of voting weighted by population, it was defeated by a vote of 32 to 33, with Harcourt casting his five votes against it.

"It was the last straw for the GVRD's regulatory role in regional planning," says Cameron. "The GVRD had overruled not only the will of the local municipality but the will of the province, and the decision was seen as a betrayal. I was told that when the minister of Municipal Affairs brought legislation to cabinet ending the planning functions of regional districts a few years later, all he had to say was, 'This bill means no more Spetifores.'"

That is not to say that urban development on the Spetifore lands was a slam dunk. Public opinion in Delta had turned against the idea, which still required changes in local zoning. Despite the expenditure of millions of dollars in staff and developers' time and the longest public hearing in the nation's history, the 2,600 homes and the golf course proposed for the site remained unbuilt. An offer to build only 1,000 homes and the golf course, providing 250 acres of foreshore for free for the park, was hooted down.

The GVRD did get the foreshore parcel it coveted as part of Boundary Bay Regional Park. In the mid-1990s, it purchased the parcel for $7.5 million, a bargain, under the Lower Mainland Nature Legacy project established by Harcourt, then premier, and his NDP government.

The Spetifore property that was excluded from the ALR continued, ironically, to be farmed rather than developed, while other lands that remain within the ALR in Delta have gone back to bush. The heritage barns, which were the only structures of value on the properties and had been touted for a new life as community centres or public facilities in an eventual new neighbourhood, became a fire hazard and had to be destroyed.

Whatever future Spetifores may await the ALR, Dave Barrett remains convinced of the land reserve's value to Greater Vancouver. "Take a look at the people who rate the livability of communities around the world. A couple of years ago Vancouver got one of the highest awards because of the 'greenbelt,' i.e., the ALR. We have a social responsibility to look to the future... This has nothing to do with political ideology. This is conceptual thinking. Any rational person who understands the population growth that will take place in this country and the need to provide land for food understands that this [farmland] must be saved. This is not just a political debate. This single issue transcends every kind of line that is drawn in our society— poor vs. rich, farmers vs. city dwellers, the political parties vs. each other. This issue affects every one of us as human beings, and if there is no sensible planning, we are the ones to blame as a community."

The Land Commission Act and the ALR have been imitated elsewhere, notably in Quebec, Ontario's Golden Horseshoe and Oregon. No subsequent B.C. government has repealed the act, although it has been almost continually tinkered with. Local appointees in each region now make the decisions about removing prime farmland from the ALR. Bob Williams, for one, favours localizing the ALR into six three-person panels, as reformatted by the present B.C. Liberal government. "It is a risk, but it's a risk in the broad sense that I favour. We should be like Switzerland and decentralize from Victoria and have macro-regions that take on most functions of the provincial government." Dave Barrett, in contrast, argues for the original centralized commission structure, saying local appointees are too susceptible to pressures in their communities.

ONGOING PRESSURE IS what the ALR is subject to and what it is designed to resolve. When a city and its rural surroundings meet at a fence, at a road, or, as is often the case in B.C., at some natural feature such as a river valley or inlet, there will be bids to develop resorts, condominiums and shopping malls. Those proposals must be weighed against the loss of a resource that takes centuries to replace. Urban land values are based upon location, location and location. Agricultural land values are based upon the land's ability to grow food for sale. As the city approaches the countryside, the potential for urban uses inflates the value of agricultural land. By confirming the long-term agricultural use of farmland, the ALR dampens this price inflation in the public interest.

By the time the ALR was established, B.C. was losing about 6,000 hectares of tillable soil each year. Since then, the size of the land reserve has remained steady at 4.7 million hectares, 5 per cent of the province's total area. The quality of soil in the reserve has declined somewhat, as prime lands are removed from the ALR and less fertile parcels, some of them at higher elevation, replace them. Guy Patterson, a planner with Smart Growth B.C., notes, "Because this limited land base supports an industry that generates $2.2 billion in direct farm income, provides at least 20,000 jobs and produces the equivalent of 50 per cent of provincial food needs, its ongoing vitality is an important public policy issue."

And not just for the sake of fresh market vegetables for city dwellers. There are other advantages the ALR brings inside the city limits. Containing a city's edges reduces infrastructure costs and encourages denser town centres, which can support such services as public transit. Then there are the views of nearby farmed hills and valleys and of forested green belts, often within the cities themselves. As byproducts of good stewardship of the land, those panoramas are irreplaceable.

Harry Lash

PLANNER WITHOUT A PLAN

HARRY LASH OPENED his book *Planning in a Human Way* with an account of a public meeting in 1975 at which he blew his stack. Lash was no ordinary planner. He was the exemplar of public participation in the planning issues of his time. What tipped him over the edge was a member of the Burnaby Citizens Association at the back of the room, yelling that the Greater Vancouver Regional District had been wasting taxpayers' money for three years to produce "a lot of baloney."

"There wasn't anything in the Livable Region proposals for Greater Vancouver that would help [the man]," Lash wrote. "He needed a house, and so did a lot of others, and what did we propose to do about it?

"He was angry—but by then, so was I. And I let it show. Nobody was going to tell me that the proposals were just baloney, not after I'd put three years of my life into them. 'Dammit,' I told him, 'they weren't baloney.' "

Whether or not the citizen of Burnaby and Lash actually used the word "baloney" is not important. Lash was certainly a gentleman most of the time. He is revered to this day by those who worked for him, but the real beneficiaries of his six years as director of planning for the GVRD were the region's citizens, the ordinary people who hadn't up to then had much of a voice in planning decisions that affected them in Greater Vancouver.

Lash felt it necessary to declare in his book that "an outburst such as mine" was unbecoming of a devoted civil servant. But he rationalized that the exchange consisted of "thoroughly human reactions... Did the meeting break up? Not at all: after that exchange, the muted hostility we had sensed all evening began to thaw. Real communication and understanding began to happen."

"Learning that I had to be myself as well as a planner was not easy for me," Lash wrote. "It would have been simpler to stick to the role of imperturbable bureaucrat, but it would not have been human." At that meeting in June 1975, he had found a way to be human and be a consummate professional at the same time. Losing his temper had its uses.

LASH WAS AN experienced planner when he came to Vancouver in 1969 from Toronto, where he had earned

a reputation for listening carefully to what neighbourhood residents had to say. That was to be his priority in
Vancouver as well. But he must have been aware that
his tenure could end at any time, over any perceived
misstep. That was what had happened to the Lower
Mainland Regional Planning Board, after all. When the
LMRPB expressed the opinion that the railway lines
ferrying coal to tidewater at Roberts Bank should con-
sume as little prime farmland as possible, W.A.C. Bennett replied by firing the board and passing its regional
planning mandate to the GVRD. Lash was recruited to
head up the new GVRD planning department.

The Bennett government finessed the extinction
of the LMRPB by using one of the oldest tricks in the
book—saying it had a better idea. In the legislation
that created regional districts in 1965, the province
gave itself the power to assign functions to the new
entities, including that of regional planning. The GVRD
was assigned this function in December 1968, setting
the stage for an order eliminating redundancy in planning functions (albeit a redundancy of the government's own creation). An order issued in March 1969
dissolved the LMRPB and transferred to the GVRD the
responsibility for administering the Official Regional
Plan within Greater Vancouver. Similar arrangements
were made for the LMRPB's plan and responsibilities
for the other three new regional districts in the Lower
Mainland: Central Fraser Valley, Dewdney-Alouette

and Fraser-Cheam. A review of this process was part of the education of Dave Zirnhelt, a researcher on regional districts who later, as an NDP cabinet minister, would observe, "Remember, the government can do anything it wants."

In any event, it was all over by the end of March 1969. Ken Cameron, then in his first year at the UBC school of planning, noticed one morning that Professor Brahm Wiesman, who would become his thesis adviser and lifelong mentor, seemed a bit out of focus. The puzzle was solved when he learned that Wiesman and several other faculty members had attended a wake for the LMRPB the night before.

HARRY LASH WAS in his late forties when he arrived on the West Coast, looking for a chance to do work that would endure. The Vancouver situation seemed in manifest need of his skills in bringing people together. Not that he had been idle in his working life to that point. After studying planning at McGill, Lash had worked in the early 1950s as a staff planner in Alberta, early in the oil boom. Next he moved east, where he worked closely with the public on two Toronto neighbourhood rezonings, in 1957 and 1959. In the mid-1960s, Lash went to Montreal to do advance work on Expo 67, which for several months that summer became the centre of the design-profession universe. In all three places Lash had found himself doing what he thought was important, useful work, only to have the documentation rolled up, rubber-banded and stacked on some archival shelf.

Lash came to B.C. for the same reason many newcomers do: to have another shot at making a difference. He was prepared to start from scratch to get the results he wanted. In that regard, Harry Lash's time as director of planning at the GVRD worked out well enough. Less than seven years elapsed between the GVRD planning department's rise from the ashes of the LMRPB and his retirement in August 1975, during which period, at the cost of his health, he revolutionized the way planning was done in the Greater Vancouver area.

Lash's approach was to start with the public's opinions, not those of his staff, and certainly not with what the regional district's politicians were asking for. On the surface a shambling, grandfatherly type, Lash was a deeply compelling, intense character and a demanding taskmaster in his professional capacity. With his thick, plastic-rimmed glasses and wavy black pompadour, he looked to be just what he was: an original, if slightly eccentric, thinker, for whom the processes of urban planning were as important—no, *more* important—than the product, or the policy package, or the program, or the strategy. "Harry was not pushy," recalls Ted Rashleigh, Lash's assistant. "You did what he wanted because you wanted to support him. You respected him, and he respected everyone."

Lash saw in the new department "an opportunity to make planning more dynamic and operational." If his claim to fame was going to be knitting together the dozen-odd separate municipalities of the GVRD, then Lash knew one thing: the plan to do so would not be recognizable as the usual zoning guide in a three-ring binder. It would be unlike any plan that had been seen before, at least in Vancouver or the Fraser Valley. And the team members who would produce this original concept would be originals themselves. As Rashleigh remembers, "Harry hired people because they had skills he needed. He didn't care about personalities, and he hired some oddball people."

Harry Lash's approach would be an interactive kind of process, in which the direction of a study or report was sometimes determined by the early conversations GVRD planners had with clients. Lash hired an American consultant on involvement techniques and worked with him for two years but decided after much soul-searching to go ahead himself, as director, and take the initiative of asking people's opinions on what issues affected them. Then, notes Rashleigh, who became Lash's in-house public involvement adviser, among his other roles, "a set of experimental meetings in 1972 established a format."

"Lash was conducting an open-ended exercise in primary democracy," says Brian Fawcett, a planner who was one of six in-house critics/second-guessers/

outreach workers appointed by Lash. "And, always, he was operating without a covert agenda or safety net. He learned, as did everyone involved... that part of the difficulty of democracy is that when citizens get used to being listened to, they begin to take themselves and their mission very seriously, and their energies and commitment to the processes they've become used to often far outstrip those of the professionals and politicians who are supposedly there to carry out their wishes."

"I seriously underestimated him," Rick Hankin confesses about his first impression of Lash. Hankin, now retired, spent his working life with the GVRD, assembling and grooming Greater Vancouver's renowned regional parks system. "He was not a colourful man, but I'll take judgement, leadership and imagination over colour anytime. He looked more like a grandfather, a schoolteacher or an academic. He shuffled and he hemmed and hawed. He spoke quite slowly, but there was tremendous power in his intellect."

Jim Wilson, who had become a planning consultant after the LMRPB was abolished, discovered it was a good idea to be thoroughly prepared for a conversation with Lash. "When you were with Harry, you didn't mess around. In professional matters he was very articulate and a very forceful person."

Harry Lash's staff regard those years as a highwater mark in their careers, time spent in almost constant innovation. Under Lash, the power balance shifted. Planners were servants of the people, as he saw it, rather than employees of their professional superiors. He insisted that his own staff—about thirty in all—were colleagues, not employees. He offered to take the fall for Leonard Minsky, the planning office's chief of public participation, whose left-wing, power-to-the-people style grated on some of the politicians on the GVRD board. For his loyalty and his innovation, Harry Lash was beatified by his colleagues. Ted Rashleigh wrote poetry in his honour.

"For two years, Lash sent his trained planners out to meet with community groups around Greater Vancouver," recalls Brian Fawcett. As a group, the six of them stayed in touch with five hundred people, "so that Harry could find out what kind of city its residents thought it should become, and what sort of specific policies they wanted in place to deal with future growth."

It turned out that, in a surprising majority of opinions, the single most important attraction of Greater Vancouver was its livability. The profession of urban planning was rocked to its foundations. Livability? How could you define livability? How much of what makes a place desirable can also make it livable? And what would it take to make Greater Vancouver a Livable Region?

LASH'S MOST IMPORTANT breakthrough was to welcome the consumers of city planning to the design table. He created what he called the Six-Sided Triangle, which symbolized the free flow of opinion, fact and questions among the public, the planners and the politicians—each of whom occupied a corner of the triangle, with the public at the top and the politicians and the planners ("or bureaucrats") at the two base corners. The idea was that information passed both ways along each side. The Six-Sided Triangle was a way of looking at public involvement, checking to see if all six connections were plugged into the current and everyone was in touch. The criterion for the right time to act was the fulfillment of what geographer and reform alderman Walter Hardwick called an "information rich environment."

"During most of the Livable Region Plan process," recalls Ted Rashleigh, "up to its conclusion, the department ran a pipeline to introduce publicly expressed local and regional issues into the [mix] and gather comments on Livable Region proposals. Especially in the early years, the Public Program"—with capital Ps— "might be considered the driver of the Livable Region Proposals. Harry was dissatisfied with producing a plan." Rashleigh explains, "His concept of planning was that it should deal with current issues in an ongoing manner."

For example, when Art Phillips became Vancouver's new mayor in 1973, Lash briefed him on the fact that the population of the Lower Mainland early in the twenty-first century was projected to be 2 to 2.5

million people. Lash's Livable Region Proposals were meant to act as the GVRD planning department's "distant early warning line," in the Cold War terminology of the day. "He had very original ideas as far as I was concerned," says Phillips today. "So I learned a great deal from him."

"We took these issues [of public concern] and subjected them to analysis—and this is another facet of Harry's creativity," Rashleigh remembers. "We put the issues in a list and then evolved a matrix with possible policy actions and a cross-impact analysis. That was a laborious task. We ended up with a very elaborate question of strength. The main outcome was to say, 'What are the strong measures to achieve that objective that have minimum impact?' "

The shock to the political and bureaucratic establishment, as Walter Hardwick characterized it, was considerable. Surprises awaited at every public information meeting. People cared enough about the Livable Region "Plan" (LRP) to fight about it. It was as if the LRP were an esoteric religious belief practised by monk-like fanatics who argued that the "Plan," quotation marks, was the escalator to a better life here on Earth. Part of their theology was that there was no actual plan. It was a time when the faithful, led by the charismatic Harry Lash, were called upon to defend their philosophy. And not necessarily by debating non-believers, although that happened often enough. Not just by yelling, although voices were often raised. No, we're talking fights here. Fisticuffs.

It was ugly. Furniture got knocked around. Livable Region information placards tumbled off easels. One man, of no fixed address, was arrested by three undercover cops who had been tipped that trouble would be in the air at the GVRD public information meeting that night. All of this happened in the Dogwood Room of the Pacific National Exhibition, March 27, 1975.

"I was afraid for a while there," remembered GVRD Chair Allan Kelly, who threw a few haymakers himself, "that my Irish blood might carry me away." He had to be restrained by individuals identified only as "regional officials."

Today, we think of Harry Lash as the father of public participation in the planning process in B.C., and the inventor of the term "livability." That night was certainly a milestone for citizen involvement in the affairs of the GVRD.

With the fracas over, Lash made his formal presentation. The greatest danger facing the future of the Livable Region Plan, he said that night, was skepticism.

IN THE END, *The Livable Region* may have been too good to be adopted. Lash oversaw the report that thirty-odd GVRD planning staff produced in 1975, a report written as the regional district's future-growth management tool. It was not the overall report local politicians had been wanting from Lash, but it was the key to a consensus on the future, with the region's politicians agreeing to accept growth targets for their municipalities. This objective, for the likes of Bill Vander Zalm, then completing his sixth year as mayor of Surrey, the fastest-growing municipality in Canada, was tantamount to handing another martini to a guy wearing a lampshade. The "decision makers," as Lash's planning staff often referred with mild irony to the politicians, wanted something a little more concrete— something they could take to the voters come November election time. The LRP was vague. It was definitely not standard procedure in Greater Vancouver to start work on a plan by asking those who would be affected how they felt about it in the abstract.

Ted Rashleigh explains. "This is the way Harry tackled it: 'This is what people are saying, so how do we deal with it? How are we going to evolve a set of policies that are satisfactory to people that we know will stand up?' It's that kind of approach that got the loyalty of the staff. The loyalty was unquestioned."

"Harry was a geographer by training," Rashleigh continues. "I would describe him as an intellectual man. He thought very carefully about things and very rationally. As the technician assigned to doing the plan, he wanted to do it as effectively, accurately and precisely as possible. And therein lies what some would say the failing of the work that was done over those years.

"I know he wasn't happy with the traditional form of planning: to develop a plan, do the research into data, population statistics, land use patterns, industrial potential, transportation routes and out of that developing a plan for twenty years into the future. That's the way we started. We hired Norman Pearson. He was a good planner. He was hired as a consultant to review all the information we had about the Greater Vancouver region and came out with a quick and dirty plan, the alpha plan. But Harry wasn't happy with that.

"Harry wasn't satisfied with that traditional form of taking the data and updating it and putting it into a new plan . . . A traditional job is to produce a document which is presented for political acceptance and then, that's it, everyone follows it. Ha, ha! Right from the beginning Harry was uncomfortable with that. He emphasized to the politicians who attended the public meetings to hear about the issues, "We don't want you to go out there and make a speech. We just want you to listen to people. No speeches. Just sit in the audience."

Lash's approach to planning was novel in another significant way, Rashleigh says. "Harry's approach was, 'How do we manage complexities?' That is not the way politicians work. They like to tackle a single issue and resolve it. So they don't like the idea of managing complexity. [But there's] this enormous, complex system that we have to make good decisions about, and we have to understand the implications of any decision we might make."

"There was a conflict about the timing and the nature of the so-called plan," recalls Art Phillips, who was plunged into the process as Vancouver's new mayor. "Harry was more concerned with establishing ongoing mechanisms instead of a blueprint, and I think he was quite right. On the other hand, we had to have some specific decisions. We as elected people were also right in pushing for conclusions to those sorts of decisions. Specifically, the Livable Region Plan involved a light rapid transit route and the creation of regional town centres."

However, says Rashleigh, Harry Lash gained the respect of the political powerhouses he worked with. "His staff was so loyal to him. Very often in a public meeting situation, I would guess he gritted his teeth. He didn't do it comfortably. At the end of the gathering, someone would throw a sticky question or complaint at him. At that time we were a team, so we were all geared up for that situation, and I can remember listening to Harry to see what kind of answer he would give to this difficult question. One could give the traditional, civil, meaningless answer. One could also give other kinds of answers, but Harry always gave the right answer. He settled that person's dissatisfaction. One of the things he said was that at public meetings, don't be a faceless civil servant. If you have an opinion as a public person, you let them know."

Ken Cameron, who was at the UBC planning school from 1968 to 1970, would join the GVRD planning staff in 1978. "I was struck by the breadth of view and the human nature of planning as Harry saw it," Cameron says. "I saw a man who had earned tremendous respect, having achieved something of lasting value that had to do with the process of planning as well as the substance of planning.

"It was Harry's belief that the GVRD board should adopt actions that would pursue the implementation of the Livable Region Plan, but that having a plan adopted by the political board was not necessary. Because the plan was not adopted, however, the legitimacy of the planning program...was never really established. So when the GVRD planning department headed into some fairly heavy weather in the late seventies and early eighties, there wasn't enough of a vessel sailing along to which people could set reference points."

Harry Lash wanted to call it a process, as in "The Plan is the Process." For him a plan was too static, too inflexible, too prone to become instantly obsolete. This *thing* he and his staff were working on had to be capable of changing the Lower Mainland as the world around it changed. What the GVRD planning committee and board of directors wanted—a zoning bylaw to specify permitted land uses—was not what Lash had in mind. Harry Lash did things the hard way. Kent Gerecke, one of the observers Lash kept around to second-guess his staff and his own leadership, once noted that Lash "was running great risks in attempting great innovation on so many fronts: a new method of planning, extensive public involvement, a non-hierarchical staff organization."

During the seven years that Harry Lash presided over planning in Greater Vancouver, the GVRD planning department would grapple with the meaning of livability. Within ten years, billions of dollars' worth of buildings were concentrated into regional town centres strung like pearls across the GVRD, the centres themselves connected by expensive SkyTrain rapid transit technology. It is testimony to Lash's acumen and artful leadership that huge investment decisions such as constructing Burnaby's Town Centre were made without even being mentioned in the Official Regional Plan left by the LMRPB. Whatever reasons developers may have had to build at sites they believed would become commercial growth engines, those reasons did not include conforming to the official plan for the GVRD, which remained mainly focussed on two-dimensional land-use designations. Nobody argues any more about whether the Livable Region strategy, or plan, or process, or whatever you want to call it, worked.

By the late summer of 1975, Lash was burned out. And no wonder. He lived twenty years longer, testimony to his toughness rather than to his health. For someone who did such important work in the Lower Fraser Basin, Harry Lash is not well remembered far beyond the present-day GVRD's headquarters. Despite the weight of the issues he confronted every working day, he was pretty much ignored by the media, too.

"He was a shy man," Rashleigh says, "incapable of small talk. He did not put people at ease very easily unless he had a reason for talking to them. He was a creative thinker. The Livable Region Plan was not just hammered together. It was started with a dissatisfaction with the way traditional planning was done. He was very well read, then exploring, becoming aware of different approaches. Out of that he hired employees you wouldn't normally hire."

The most notable reminder of Harry Lash's presence is his name on the door of the Harry Lash Library at the GVRD offices. His short textbook, *Planning in a Human Way* (1976), is much quoted and has extended his influence well past his death in August 1995. Lash ends his book on a generous note with a quote from Jim Wilson's memoir, *People in the Way:* "Does this imply that every planner would have to be a paragon of compassion, objectivity and firmness? It does. It also means that it is impossible for planning to be completely trouble-free. There just are not enough saints to go around."

Greater Vancouver remains, to this day, without an overall land-use bible. What Harry Lash left behind instead were the essentials of planning theory in a singular setting: a dense waterfront in the City of Vancouver, which anchors a string of regional town centres extending eastward and linked by rapid transit. Not bad for a planner without a plan.

Expo 86 and
the Remaking of
False Creek

THE GROUNDBREAKING FOR Vancouver's rapid transit system was a quiet ceremony, carried out under leaden skies and a huddle of dripping black umbrellas near the intersection of Terminal Avenue and Station Street in early 1982. Despite the presence of Premier Bill Bennett, the always incandescent minister of Tourism, Grace McCarthy, and the usual Social Credit hangers-on, the gathering struck an observer as more funereal than celebratory. There had been arguments over the light rail linear-induction power technology and over the route chosen to be the first of an eventual region-wide system. Buying the unproven hardware, however discounted in price, had pretty much committed Vancouver to buy more of the same for future routes. For some of those present, both the hardware and the route were personal defeats.

This was Grace McCarthy's show. During the fall of 1978 she had asked Ambassador Patrick Reid of Canada House about the possibility of borrowing the *Mona Lisa* to be showcased for Vancouver's 1986 centennial. Reid had another idea. As it happened, he was also president of the International Bureau of Expositions, the organization responsible for choosing world's fair locations. "Why couldn't Vancouver have one?" McCarthy inquired at their meeting. Reid replied, "Because it has never asked." That had set in motion the process leading to this groundbreaking ceremony. The French were never going to lend Vancouver the *Mona Lisa,* but there was a Canadian-built rapid transit system looking for a place to demonstrate its fast, quiet technology.

The 1982 gathering marked a historic moment. The schemes of uncounted transportation planning consultants were about to take shape as reinforced concrete above the grass boulevard of Terminal Avenue. The hopes of the Livable Region Plan would become likelihoods with rapid transit. The SkyTrain, which operated without drivers, would link the regional town centres that were the GVRD's strategy for managing population growth within the region. The new system's trade name had a certain ring to it; it was derived from that of the SeaBus, the Burrard Inlet passenger ferry.

Of the couple dozen rain-coated VIPs on hand, two seemed alienated from the rest. One of those was Dick Mann, a partner with the city's most important firm of architects, Thompson, Berwick, Pratt and Partners, who had laid out the first SkyTrain route. A reporter who knew the talented urban designer suspected he had created the east-west alignment under political pressure; Mann refused to answer questions from journalists about the system. He pulled his collar up and his hat brim down, looking for all the world like a turtle standing on its hind feet. The light rail route that was about to be built was not the one Mann thought should be constructed first.

The other, taller lone figure was well known to everyone present. He was Mike Harcourt, the thirty-ninth mayor of Vancouver. Harcourt favoured a bigger, higher-capacity system that would go underground for the southbound stretch along Commercial Drive and would be driven by an operator. He welcomed the small stampede of reporters curious to know why he was standing so far apart from the other dignitaries. Flashing a grin, he replied, "I wasn't invited."

UP TO THE moment Premier Bennett dug the first shovelful and the SkyTrain project was officially underway, Mike Harcourt had consistently pointed out that Vancouver was in danger of hosting a second-tier world's fair celebrating transportation while itself running a third-rate public transit system. As a Vancouver city councillor, Harcourt had been lukewarm to Expo when the idea became public in 1980.

Nevertheless, he was not as black or white on either Expo 86 or the SkyTrain as some people thought. Harcourt preferred to get things done, and he took pride in being able to work with anyone who could help. He had studied the financial disaster that was Montreal's 1976 Olympic Games. (Montreal's share of the $1.2 billion deficit was $300 million, which would take that city thirty years to repay, along with $1 billion in principal and interest charges.) Harcourt thought Expo 86 would run an overall deficit itself, and on some of its keynote facilities. In his bid to become mayor the following year, he campaigned on a platform of no exposition unless six conditions were met: no debt for the city, the site assembled, rapid transit in place, security provided, tenants protected and traffic management systems in operation.

Once elected, Harcourt used his office to hammer home the idea that although the province owned the proposed Expo site—the north shore of False Creek east of the Granville Street Bridge—it did not have the power to ignore the city's floor-space limits on the buildings to be constructed after the world's fair. (The province probably did have that power, but exercising it would have been a political disaster for the Socreds.) And just because it had been McCarthy's idea to host a world's fair in Vancouver's centennial year, Harcourt said, that didn't mean carte blanche on the important land-use issues that arose from the Expo 86 proposal and whatever would be built on the site afterward.

FALSE CREEK SOUTH, the housing development directly across False Creek from the proposed Expo site, was more indicative of the state of design in 1980s Vancouver than the splashy but mostly design-formatted world's fair would be. The nations, companies and districts mounting exhibits at the fair would rent space in pavilions assembled from standard kits. False Creek South was innovative in every possible way, and you needed no ticket to see something truly original. If there was any single project that announced that Vancouver had a leading-edge planning culture and the architects to build highly livable mixed-market and non-market housing, False Creek South was it. The first part of False Creek to be developed for housing was a natural bowl facing north with views past the downtown peninsula, curving from the Granville Street Bridge to the Cambie Street Bridge. False Creek South was dense for a Vancouver neighbourhood built in the 1970s, but the density was mostly low-rise and was contained in clustered row houses styled and landscaped to mask their mass.

Walter Hardwick, the first of the reform councillors from The Electors' Action Movement (TEAM) to be elected to Vancouver city council in 1968, had studied the industrial sewer that was False Creek in minute detail. Hardwick, working with architect Wolfgang Gerson, assigned students in his 1965 UBC geography class to look the area over and rough out some ideas. Hardwick took his own children, in oversized gumboots, to the inlet's fetid edges to get a whiff of the possibilities that lay beneath the obsolete barrel works and chain-making forest-industry support companies that dominated False Creek's shores. It would take a radical change of mindset among the city's senior planners to lose their fondness for False Creek's outdated lumber mills with their iron-age jobs, each mill with a beehive burner that kept the air above the inlet perpetually smoggy. Only when planners were ordered by TEAM councils in the early 1970s to approach the basin with an open mind did the plan for a city-centre home for 30,000 people develop, with micro neighbourhoods designed by Vancouver's leading architectural firms, among them Henriquez and Todd, Rhone and Iredale, and Thompson, Berwick, Pratt and Partners.

Thirty thousand was not enough for NDP MLA Bob Williams; he thought more density might have sustained a higher frequency of public transit in and out of the development. But the level of density along False Creek's south shore was decided by one of the first, most complete and most inclusive public participation processes seen up to then in Vancouver. The possibilities for False Creek presented to the public ranged from nothing but sports fields and community services to family-oriented high-density residential. The responders got what most of them wanted— mainly residential development as part of a mix of uses. Completed in 1977, the development would go on to win awards for the most original water-oriented, inner-city development of its time.

False Creek South's most important characteristic was the diversity of its residents. Walter Hardwick realized that if Vancouver stayed on its course of the 1970s, it would become an "executive city," driving average income earners out of the Vancouver real estate market. The formula for the False Creek South development was fixed at one-third low income, one-third medium income (mostly co-ops) and one-third market housing. This requirement for mixed incomes was one of the features, along with the compactness of the development's urban design, making possible a "generosity of open space" that John Punter praises in *The Vancouver Achievement* as "almost utopian." Vancouver's mayor at the time, investment guru Art Phillips, promptly moved into a waterfront unit. The principle of including varied incomes in developments built on city property was set, and it remains in force in Vancouver today, a memorial to Walter Hardwick and his small complement of builders, notably engineer Doug Sutcliffe, who were committed to making "urban renewal" work for everyone.

In hindsight, the flaw in False Creek South was its exclusion of cars. Aside from its access road, the area has narrow or exclusively pedestrian/bicycle streets and pathways. Unfortunately, the public transit promised to residents there, a captive ridership of 30,000 people, never fully materialized.

THE NORTH SHORE of False Creek evolved along very different lines. B.C. Place (BCP), the Crown corporation set up to develop the former CP Rail yard that stretched the shore's length, had a history of reminding civic staff and politicians that, as the instrument of a more senior level of government, it was not bound by the city's zoning bylaws. Nor, for that matter, was BCP bound by the system of floor-space bonuses under which City Hall awarded additional height in return for such public amenities as the False Creek waterfront walkway and the restoration of the CPR Roundhouse, surely one of the top five historic buildings in Vancouver. BCP wanted it down. The Roundhouse's future was assured only after UBC architecture students stood before the bulldozers in November 1981.

B.C. Place made two serious urban design errors in its stewardship of the 82.5-hectare Expo site before the party ever got started.

The first big mistake was Pacific Boulevard. The four- to six-lane would-be speedway was a source of great personal pride for Paul Manning, B.C. Place's vice president of public affairs. He argued that Pacific Boulevard, the first newly built object on the site in 1980–81, would provide a much-needed scenic shortcut through the pre-Expo railyard wasteland. That

depended on which direction you happened to be driving. The route westbound between B.C. Place Stadium
and the downtown escarpment is still a dank near-
tunnel, thanks to the decision to split the road to pass
the stadium on both sides instead of running a single
roadway along the stadium's south side. Pacific Boulevard was an exercise in short-sightedness: there is a big
difference between a road built in a near-empty landscape and that same road years later in a high-density,
high-rise community. From the beginning, the route
was designed for cars rather than the pedestrians
now using the crosswalks, which are mini-marathons
for the elderly or the disabled. Visually, the width of
Pacific Boulevard is way over scale, even with the high-
rise buildings of Concord Pacific later set on streetwall
podiums on either side. The boulevard slices the Yaletown neighbourhood in two. And the route is down-
right dangerous for drivers at its east and west ends,
where bumper-to-bumper traffic must criss-cross with
vehicles coming off bridge ramps.

BCP's second mistake was the design of 1983's B.C.
Place Stadium, the sheer bulk of which overwhelms
its human-scaled heritage surroundings. The souve-
nir program for the first B.C. Lions game played under
the dome said that the stadium would be "the object
of envy across the country." That may have been
true across the country, and it was also true that the
dome brought B.C. Lions' football indoors from the

quagmires of Empire Stadium. But in doing so, it excluded what little and precious sunlight Vancouver receives during autumn. An exact copy of Minnesota's dome, which was designed for a harsher climate, Vancouver's also seals spectators off from those crisp fall days that offer ideal football weather. On the inside, B.C. Place Stadium is a characterless engineered building. Its plaza remains empty all but a dozen or so times a year. Part of the rationale for a quilt-top stadium was to make major-league baseball playable in Vancouver during the monsoons. Instead, people still prefer to watch A-level ball at Nat Bailey Stadium, a park where you can watch the sun set from the third-base box seats.

As Vancouver mayor, backed by a shaky single-vote majority in favour of his centre-left coalition on city council, Mike Harcourt had a fine line to tread throughout the Expo design-build cycle. In the run-up to the election, Harcourt had predicted a $50 million deficit on the Canadian pavilion proposed for Expo 86. The pavilion would cost no more than $25 million, McCarthy retorted, and she called Harcourt a liar. Two weeks after Harcourt was elected mayor, McCarthy called a press conference at the Hotel Vancouver to announce the pavilion's projected cost was $100 million.

In response, Harcourt appointed an aldermanic task force consisting of hard-nosed George Puil, courtroom terrier Harry Rankin and the charming but knife-edged May Brown to negotiate a deal with BCP. The committee demanded and got immunity for the city from the Expo debt in exchange for the city exempting Canada Harbour Place, as the Expo 86 Canadian pavilion and future convention complex was named, from the $600,000 to $1 million annual charges for water, sewers, fire and police protection. Harcourt credits Senator Jack Austin for stickhandling the Canada Harbour Place proposal through the Trudeau cabinet. Retrofitted after Expo to a trade and conference centre and cruise-ship dock at a cost of $200 million, Canada Harbour Place repaid that investment in five years, Harcourt says today, "a win/win/win situation if there ever was one."

Issues related to the Cambie Street Bridge deepened the city's continuing argument with the province. It was generally agreed that a new Cambie bridge was essential to serve as a link with the Expo site from the West Broadway area. However, Harcourt did not want to accept what looked like a political gift from the province—one-quarter of the price of a new bridge—as long as problems with BCP still needed sorting out. Many of these problems were minor irritations, but there were also important questions such as setting the exact location of the False Creek north-shore water's edge and walkway and establishing who would pay for removing the contaminated soil on the site. Even once those issues were resolved, in some cases with an agreement not to agree, Harcourt's sometime allies from the Committee of Progressive Electors reiterated their opposition to anything connected with Expo 86, including the bridge. Harcourt trumped them by having the matter referred to a citywide referendum, in which voters overwhelmingly approved a new bridge.

By 1984 a shortage of goodwill was looming between Expo and its closest neighbours. The situation could not be quantified as precisely as the money being spent on Expo 86 buildings and programming; in this case, something beyond calculation was at stake—the emotional cost to people of being evicted from their living spaces. Vancouver's Downtown Eastside bordered the Expo site on the north and east perimeters, close enough for the smell of cash to drift across the property line to the flophouses and their owners. Is there an index to measure the level of desperation that attends the eviction of, say, a fifty-eight-year-old retired logger on disability who has eaten and slept in the same room for twenty-five years?

"In the past four years, about eighty private rooming houses—which provided more than two thousand rooms for low-income families and individuals—have closed down," Harcourt informed the media in 1984, citing social planners' figures. "Some have been converted to non-residential use; others have been demolished."

Others interested in Expo's eviction effect did their own calculations. Kris Olds's study for the Centre for

Human Settlements at UBC entitled *Canada: Hallmark Events, Evictions and Housing Rights* cited community activists' estimates ranging from "a few" to 2,000 evictees. Olds used a variety of sources to arrive at his own estimate of between 500 and 850 evictions leading up to the 1986 hallmark event. He added that a further 1,000 to 1,500 sleeping/housekeeping units were switched from monthly rental to tourist rental during the spring of 1986. Jim Green, then president of the Downtown Eastside Residents Association, has stated that eleven people died as a result of being evicted. Three, he said, were suicides.

Harcourt and his fragile civic coalition took the Expo evictions seriously, leveraging from the world's fair a program of buying and renovating single-room occupancy hotels to add to the city's low-income housing stock.

"HOW THE CITY has changed," a reporter mused to Harcourt on Expo's last day, before writing a story that appeared under the headline "Expo Legacy Includes Pride, Hope for Future." Harcourt reminded the reporter that the citizens of Vancouver had changed as well. "We are no longer trying to be someone else," he said. "We are proud of what we are."

It took seventeen thousand artisans and tradespeople to build and staff Expo 86, including nine thousand construction jobs over three years. There were opportunities for graphic artists, high-end printers, landscape architects, ad agencies, filmmakers and music producers. The whole package cost $1.6 billion, twice the estimated $800 million price. There was a deficit, Expo CEO Jimmy Pattison claimed afterward, of "slightly under $311 million." Harcourt estimated the actual Expo 86 deficit was more than twice that amount, nearly $800 million. The difference was in what you included, such as the $144.8 million spent on the Canada Harbour Place pavilion before it was converted to a convention centre and cruise ship facility. The overall economic impact of Expo on B.C.'s economy, which had gone south in the early to mid-1980s, was calculated at $7 billion. There were twenty-two million visits to the site.

The usual measure of an exposition's lasting value is a list of what have become known as "legacies," or facilities built for the fair. The truly oddball success among the Expo legacies is Science World, which attracted much derision when it was completed as the Expo Preview Centre in 1985. Its architectural merits notwithstanding, its location at the head of False Creek makes it one of those reference-point landmarks to which people become attached. Seen from farther east, it is the most recognizable building among many in the new, eastward-migrating downtown. Seen from any of the False Creek bridges, it locates you with less fuss than a hand-held GPS. Science World is the best-known building of Expo architect Bruno Freschi's distinguished Vancouver portfolio. Nobody asks how much it cost to build ($22 million).

But as the *Vancouver Sun*'s Pete McMartin wrote in 1996, after ten years of mulling over the question, Expo's greatest legacy might not be buildings at all. The Expo 86 that Arthur Erickson complained had blackballed him was never intended to be much of an architectural showcase. Bruno Freschi conceived a very imaginative layout, including a waterway through Chinatown and Gastown that would have restored the connection between False Creek and the harbour along Columbia Street at high tide each half day. When the second management under Pattison took over from the originals, the emphasis became getting the job done on time.

For Vancouver, the newly minted cultural dynamo and emerging information-age switchboard, the greatest legacy might be the perspectives of outsiders such as the *New Yorker*'s E.J. Kahn, who looked at Vancouver, in McMartin's view, "from outside the fish bowl... [and] allowed us, for the first time, to see ourselves as others might see us."

Not only the good stuff, the beaches and the mountains, but the pitchmen who brought to the affair, McMartin wrote, "chauvinism and smug, small-town babbittry, too. It was a passage of sorts, a coming out party for a backwater."

In the fourteen years before 1986, 9 to 11 per cent of international visitors to Canada came to B.C. During 1986, B.C.'s share was more than 17 per cent, and over the following fourteen years, that share increased from 12 per cent in 1987 to 17 per cent in 2000. Tourism now adds $9 billion annually to the province's economy. And people want to move to the province as well. In the decade after 1986, the population of B.C. grew at the rate of sixty to eighty thousand persons a year, an 18 per cent overall increase.

Mike Harcourt got some of the benefits from Expo 86 he was looking for as mayor. Today, he points not only to the $600 million original SkyTrain route, but to Expo megaprojects such as Canada Harbour Place and the redevelopment of the Expo site by Concord Pacific.

The first SkyTrain line will endure as a regional-planning milestone with both good and worrisome features. SkyTrain was a discounted gift from the province—marked down! only $600 million!—a demo model intended to sell similar hardware in places like Bangkok. Among its shortcomings are rush-hour overloads (because this is light rapid transit), and the menacing gloom of the Broadway and New Westminster stations and the barren Stadium stop. The Expo Line imposed itself on Commercial Drive south of Broadway, its piers looming over the community. Harcourt offered to have the city foot half the bill to put that stretch of the system underground, but the province didn't see the point.

As for the Expo site, Harcourt would have handled the redevelopment process differently, he says. He would have broken the site down into smaller parcels so that local developers could have taken parts of the action, using False Creek South as the model. By the time Harcourt was premier of B.C. and might have had some influence, however, the decision to sell the site as a single property, to Concord Pacific, had long since been made. Marathon Realty, CP Rail's landowning subsidiary, had assembled the site but did not have the wherewithal to develop it. Marathon's project manager at the time was Gordon Campbell, a developer who had served as executive assistant to Vancouver mayor Art Phillips and as a former Vancouver city councillor. Even as connected a player as Campbell couldn't raise the money required to close the deal on North False Creek. Meanwhile, architect Stanley Kwok was at work during Expo figuring out how to make the site work while fronting enough money to develop two major parks and the shoreline walkway before there was any cash flow from sales of condominiums. Soon after Expo, Victor Li, son of billionaire Li Ka-shing, was working with Kwok to polish their scheme for the huge tract. First-class firms of architects, starting with Rick Hulbert's resort specialists, joined the effort. Since the sale of the site for the much-criticized bargain price of $145 million to the Hong Kong magnate, the city has ceased to hear about issues with the project. Perhaps that has to do with nothing more than the ability of one of the world's richest men to get Concord Pacific built without glitches. Then again, there was the unprecedented co-operative planning process that had city planners working with such distinguished Concord Pacific consultants as landscape architect Don Vaughn. Vaughn had a lot to do with the towers' vital ground-plane treatments. Where a tower emerges from the earth, it takes flair to make the immediate surroundings look natural.

In housing twenty thousand people, the Concord Pacific project has been the key to increasing the population living in Vancouver's downtown by one third. Housing so many people in the heart of the city is the centrepiece of the Livable Region Strategy. What was more difficult to foresee, but fortuitous, was the near-instant strong identity of specific neighbourhoods within the project. Yaletown not only knits the old warehouse district with new high-rise brick fascia construction, but it also has focal points that generate off-hours activity despite storefronts as yet unrented along Pacific Boulevard.

THE CAMBIE STREET Bridge is seldom listed as an Expo legacy, but it may be the one Mike Harcourt is most proud of. The province eventually declined to participate in financing the bridge; Expo contributed $12 million, and the city raised $40 million on the basis of 76 per cent support for the bridge in a capital-works referendum. Expo's participation was sealed by the transfer of some city-owned parcels of land that everyone agreed should be incorporated into the Expo site at its eastern end. Bridges are a big deal in Vancouver, for obvious reasons. But this one was special, because Harcourt put together the vote to proceed on it councillor by councillor.

The Cambie Bridge, which made city engineer Bill Curtis the most recent member of the city engineers' exclusive "Bridge Club," came in at an unbelievable 25 per cent under budget and was completed an even more impressive seven months ahead of schedule. Moreover, Curtis considered the Cambie Bridge an engineering masterpiece, something close to a structural work of art, starting with the carefully selected warm taupe-coloured concrete it is built of. The grand but gentle rise of the piers at each end make the crossing the easiest in the region for cyclists and pedestrians; the Cambie Bridge is the only way to cross False Creek without a vehicle and feel safe. The bridge also made the boulevard rising from Sixth Avenue to City Hall a ceremonial prospect totally absent when the bridge was held up by rusty iron with boards for a deck. Harcourt, former Expo skeptic, used the bridge proposal to leverage a provincial guarantee that the city would be off the hook for any Expo 86 deficit. The province established Lotto 6/49 to take care of that.

Choosing Our Future

GORDON CAMPBELL SPREADS

HIS POLITICAL WINGS

EXPO 86 AND the surge of growth that followed
it cured the crisis of self-confidence that British
Columbia had suffered during the near-depression of
the early 1980s. By 1988 it was possible to believe that
the terrible economic, social and political events of the
first part of the decade were an aberration rather than,
as Social Credit Premier Bill Bennett had called them,
a "new reality."

In fact, there was increasing concern that growth
itself could be a major threat to the quality of life in
the province. For many in the Lower Mainland, this
threat was most graphically illustrated by the seem-
ingly overnight transformation of large areas such as
Mary Hill in Port Coquitlam from treed hills to single-
family subdivisions with massive homes and no trees.
People became concerned about the impact of growth

on the region's transportation system, on rivers and streams and on community services.

In early 1988 the GVRD board decided to beef up its planning capabilities to respond to this challenge. It was a decision that would need some delicacy in its implementation. Memories were vivid of the place of regional planning in the "restraint" program, the Bill Bennett government's attack on the public sector following the election of 1983, which had brought the province to the brink of a general strike. Included among the twenty-six "restraint" bills was an act removing regional planning as a function of regional districts and cancelling all official regional plans. The GVRD had kept the embers of planning alive by means of a voluntary contract with the fifteen member municipalities to deliver "development services," the advisory, knowledge-based component. Although the 1976 Livable Region Proposals lived on in the hearts and minds of many, the contractual arrangement with the municipalities was inherently unstable, and the GVRD's planning capability was dying a slow death.

Responding to the board's wishes, the GVRD's new regional manager, Mike O'Connor (fresh from managing the construction of what is now called the Expo SkyTrain line), created an opening for a new department head. Interest in the position when it was advertised was minimal. Ken Cameron, considered by many to be the dauphin regional planning director, didn't even apply. "I was making more money and having more fun as the city planner for New Westminster," he recalls. "It was real city building in a community that wanted progress. You'd work with developers on plans for Westminster Quay, the B.C. Penitentiary site or the western Fraser River waterfront, take them to council and through the public process, then see buildings coming out of the ground a few months later. The new developments increased New Westminster's population by 10 per cent between 1985 and 1990 and made it a better place to live, work and shop. We demonstrated that the challenge is not growth itself, but how it is managed."

O'Connor revised the remuneration for the position, and Cameron applied when it was advertised a second time. He remembers the selection process as being pretty speedy. "I think I was by far the most suitable candidate in Mike's mind," he said. In that magic moment between an employment offer being made but not yet accepted, Cameron negotiated some provisions that would begin to restore the position of the development services department, including confirmation that he would be a manager with the same status as the other GVRD managers, notwithstanding the department's modest budget and staff, which by then had shrunk to seven people. "It was a graphic illustration of how near the unit was to death," Cameron says. "There was literally nowhere to go but up." When

Cameron left the GVRD sixteen years later, the policy and planning department would have 135 staff and be responsible for planning for growth management, for water, for liquid waste management, for solid waste management and for the GVRD's entire air quality management function.

O'Connor took a bit of a beating when he informed the GVRD board of Cameron's appointment. Some members, including the up-and-coming young mayor of Vancouver, Gordon Campbell, thought the board should have been involved in the selection of a new manager. They were, after that.

O'Connor's inspired response to Campbell's interest was to persuade the board chair, Richmond mayor Gil Blair, to offer Mayor Campbell the position of chair of the development services committee, which was formed to oversee the resurrection of regional planning. Campbell's acceptance brought with it his commitment to use the position to respond constructively to the increasing concern about growth. Taking this on, while he was not only mayor of Vancouver but also moving up through the leadership ranks of the Union of British Columbia Municipalities (UBCM), said a lot about his capacity, his drive and his ambition.

GVRD staff readily agreed to Campbell's suggestion that Dr. Walter Hardwick be retained as the "convener" of a process to address the future of the region. Hardwick not only brought valuable experience from the creation of the Livable Region Proposals in the 1970s, but he also had a towering reputation and an eclectic imagination—and he enjoyed Campbell's utter confidence.

In his message at the memorial service for Hardwick in 2005, Campbell would say, "For me, Walter will always be a teacher. Standing in front of the lecture hall, standing in front of his red council chair in Vancouver's council chambers, hands moving, bow tie brimming with colour at his chin, teaching us all to think beyond ourselves and what is to what could be. Opening our eyes to possibility."

Thus began the Choosing Our Future process. Today we know this process as "agenda development," an apt demonstration of how jargon can suck meaning and energy from good concepts. Later, British Columbians would see Campbell's approach reflected in the *New Era Document* that formed the platform for his election to the premier's chair in 2001 and in the *Five Great Goals for a Golden Decade* for his re-election in 2005.

All of these processes had trademark "agenda development" features:

· A multi-faceted approach to getting input: In the case of Choosing Our Future, there were research studies, opinion surveys, "challenge seminars," a children's poster contest and public meetings.

- A broad focus and future orientation: The challenge seminars organized by Hardwick demonstrated the project's sweeping scope: social inclusion, urban design, justice, transportation and the environment.

- Intensiveness: Choosing Our Future went from a standing start in December 1989 to a finished product adopted by the GVRD board in July 1990.

- Private sector engagement: McDonald's restaurants sponsored the children's poster contest; the editor of the *Vancouver Sun* was astonished to find the mayor of Vancouver standing on his front doorstep at the dinner hour trying to get the *Sun* to participate.

- Value-based propositions: Choosing Our Future uncovered deep public support for value-based concepts such as the Green Zone and a transportation system that gives priority to walking, cycling and goods movement ahead of the private automobile.

- A commitment to be accountable for results: As Choosing Our Future unfolded, Campbell and GVRD staff began to describe the eventual outcome as a document called *Creating Our Future*, which would contain specific goals and targets against which progress could be measured.

THE PROCESS GOT underway in earnest in January 1990. Some changes in senior management at the

GVRD altered the context in which it took place. Mike O'Connor had succumbed to the direct wooing of Rita Johnston, British Columbia's minister responsible for transit, to become chief executive officer of B.C. Transit. His replacement was Ben Marr, a man with many years of experience in environmental management, most recently as British Columbia's deputy minister of Forests and deputy minister of Environment, Lands and Parks. Creation within the GVRD of a new department of communications and education and the recruitment of a new manager for the department, Judy Kirk, brought into play one of the province's shrewdest, most strategic professionals in public consultation and communications.

"Judy was the perfect addition to our team," Cameron says today. "She was brilliant at identifying the messages that evoke buy-in. The best example of this to me was the way she opened a meeting between the GVRD and the editorial board of the *Vancouver Sun* with 'We serve the same people.' It was all she needed to say."

"It was a hectic time, and a situation that could have resulted in disaster," Cameron remembers. "With the exception of Walter and Gordon, none of us had even known each other six months before we launched Choosing Our Future. It could have flown apart, but instead it forged friendships and partnerships that have lasted for the rest of our lives."

The challenge seminars were uniquely designed to facilitate learning and dialogue between local leaders and a well-known outside expert. With Hardwick as the chair, the day would begin with the presentation of information about the subject matter (e.g., transportation, demographic trends, etc.) in the Greater Vancouver context. "This part of the seminars got people on the same page," recalls Cameron. "Walter's reverence for knowledge created an almost sacramental aura around the consumption of this information, and the consideration of it in the presence of an outside expert enhanced the importance of the process, particularly for the elected people." At lunch, the invited expert would make a presentation on his or her particular area of expertise, not specifically related to Greater Vancouver. Then, at the end of the day, the expert would be asked to blend his or her own expertise with what he or she had learned about Greater Vancouver's specific situation and offer some advice.

The defining moment in Choosing Our Future came during one of the challenge seminars. The guest was Bonnie Menes Kahn, author of *Cosmopolitan Culture: The Gilt-edged Dream of a Tolerant City*. "I was never sure whether the right term was 'gilt-edged' or 'guilt-edged,'" says Cameron with a laugh today. "In any event, what she said rang like a bell. Having studied the elements that have made cities great, she had reached two important conclusions. The first was that greatness was a function of the extent to which cities welcomed newcomers and incorporated their talents into city life. Shakespeare was not from London; Mozart was not from Vienna. As a region already among the most diverse in the world, with a third of our residents born outside of Canada, Greater Vancouver had an opportunity rather than a problem here. The second idea was that each city had one or more moments in time when it developed or discovered something of universal importance for humanity. Athens and democracy. Vienna and music. London and the theatre. At the end of the day, someone in the audience asked Bonnie when and for what such a moment might come for Vancouver. She said, 'Now— for growing past 2 million people while making your city better, gaining something, not losing things that make your city livable.' We could have our cake and eat it too."

It was the inspiration for what became the Creating Our Future vision.

As the process moved towards the end of its schedule, GVRD staff, Hardwick and Campbell began to consider what it revealed about the future the people of Greater Vancouver were after. Walter Hardwick's opinion research was providing some very interesting information. People's values about the protection of livability and environmental quality had not been shaken by the economic shocks of the early 1980s—

they wanted a healthy economy, but not at any cost. A substantial percentage said they agreed with the statement that "getting to work is not a particular problem for me," an indication that transportation issues, while important, were not the urgent concern that the media often made them.

After Campbell, Hardwick, Cameron and GVRD senior planner Hugh Kellas completed some intensive Saturday discussions at Hardwick's Kitsilano Point home, GVRD staff started to pull together a draft document entitled *Creating Our Future*. The moment of truth was approaching: could these policy wonks collaborate?

Campbell took the draft with him on a twentieth-anniversary getaway to the Gulf Islands with his wife, Nancy. When he returned, he had cut and pasted pieces of the draft, plus his own material, into a three-hole coil UBC notebook. The well-ordered but dull draft document had been converted into an inspirational, value-driven agenda for the region.

Or at least it was getting there. Cameron could see that more work was needed to get to a final product, and he was unsure whether Campbell was passing the pen back with his draft. "We didn't know whether we were to treat the notebook as a set of stone tablets or whether we were able to take the material and polish it into something more complete. Fortunately, it turned out to be the latter," he says.

Today, Cameron is proudest of the document's vision statement, which he drafted as follows:

> Greater Vancouver can become the first city in the world to combine in one place the things to which humanity aspires on a global basis: a place where human activities enhance rather than degrade the natural environment, where the quality of the built environment approaches that of the natural setting, where the diversity of origins and religions is a source of social strength rather than strife, where people control the destiny of their community, and where the basics of food, clothing, shelter, security and useful activity are accessible to all.

BASED ON BONNIE Menes Khan's stunning guidance, this vision was aspirational about what the city could become if it tried, and it highlighted the astonishing fact that no other city had been able to achieve rapid growth without losing livability. No citizen of Greater Vancouver would accept such an outcome if they had the opportunity to make the choice, and now they did.

"We took the vision statement to the development services committee ahead of the rest of the document," Cameron says. "They made only one change—to replace the word 'city' with the words 'urban region,' a move that said so much about the need to see Vancouver's future from a regional perspective. Later, Gordon

Campbell told a group that he hadn't written the vision statement but he wished he had. That was quite an admission from a man about whom it had been said that there are two kinds of ideas in Gordon Campbell's world—there are Gordon Campbell's ideas and then there's shit."

The traditional way for the GVRD board to make an important decision was to receive it first and refer it to the member municipalities for comment before acting. Campbell wasn't having any of that with *Creating Our Future*. He got the board to approve the document first. When staff expressed concerns about how such an apparent *fait accompli* might be received by the municipal councils, he said, "I'll go out and explain it to them."

Thus began the first of several road shows Campbell made as GVRD chair to visit the by-then twenty municipal councils affiliated with the GVRD in their chambers. At that time, all councils except Vancouver met on Monday nights. With the able assistance of David Cadman, now a Vancouver city councillor but at that time a staff member in the communications and education department, visits were scheduled to all the councils in five weeks, sometimes five in one evening. Campbell, Cameron and Judy Kirk made the visits in Cameron's blue Pontiac 6000 station wagon. The timing was so tight that Cameron resolved to have remote keyless entry on his vehicle by the time

of the next such undertaking, to prevent Campbell
from tearing the door handle off in his haste to get
to the next meeting. The visits started on October 15
in a year in which Campbell was up for re-election on
November 17, and once or twice Cameron had to pick
the mayor up from campaign events.

Campbell made the presentation to each council,
honing the messages and shaping them to respond
to feedback from the councillors. No GVRD chair had
ever made such an effort to connect with the member
councils. In the car between stops, Kirk would give
feedback on the messaging, leaning forward from the
back seat. Campbell would fake sobs of grief if she
was too hard on him. Together, Campbell, Cameron
and Kirk would talk about ideas for making the GVRD
work better.

The conversations with the councils, and in the
car, underlined the GVRD's fundamental nature
as a municipal federation, *one* system of local government, not two as in other regional governance
models, in which most of the business is done by the
member municipalities with some responsibilities del-
egated upward to the regional level. Campbell treated
all members of council as respected constituents—
equals—rather than dealing solely with the people
who represented their municipalities on the GVRD
board. Further conversation in the Pontiac led to the
concept of holding meetings from time to time of all

the municipally elected people in the region to talk about common issues. This Council of Councils is now a regional institution.

As the process continued, it became clearer and clearer that there was no place in Campbell's concept of the GVRD for a superior/subordinate relationship between the GVRD and its members. "We need to focus on the things we can agree on," he argued. "By the time we've dealt with those things, we will have run out of time to discuss the things we disagree on." It was a non-partisan, inclusive style that was relatively rare in local politics, where councillors' loyalties to provincial and federal political parties always lurk in the shadows. It also meant that decisions would have to be made by consensus. To Cameron, that seemed a tall order, considering the vexatious issues of growth management and transportation that were looming in the region.

Cameron and Campbell also differed over the long-standing idea that Greater Vancouver should have a regional economic strategy. Reacting to former Vancouver mayor Mike Harcourt's globetrotting approach to economic development, Campbell said, "Local government can't do anything about economic development. It's just trips." Cameron couldn't convince the mayor that if an urban region had issues and opportunities in planning and development, there were probably economic issues and opportunities that should be addressed as well. Given British Columbia's status as a small, open economy whose opportunities lay in the Asia Pacific, a certain amount of relationship-building travel might be helpful, Cameron argued to no avail. "We slipped some economic stuff into later versions of *Creating Our Future,* Cameron says today. "But it never amounted to much."

By the end of the road show, *Creating Our Future* had been validated as the agenda for the region. In the process, Campbell had also equipped himself for a bid to succeed Gil Blair as chair of the GVRD board, a position in which he first demonstrated his ability to lead other elected people to astonishing achievements. Updated in 1993 and 1996, *Creating Our Future* provided the vision and direction for the region for the better part of a decade, long after Gordon Campbell had moved to the provincial scene as leader of the B.C. Liberal party. He was joined there by Judy Kirk, who served as executive director of the Liberal caucus in a partnership that was incubated in Cameron's blue station wagon.

"When I look back on it, I'm amazed at what we accomplished in just under a year," Cameron says today. "Both Gordon and Judy were new to the GVRD, and the new chief administrative officer, Ben Marr, was willing to support a process that was working. My wife and I had a new baby at home. Gordon and I had some similarities in our backgrounds—both from Vancouver's west side, both left fatherless at a young age and having to take on family responsibilities to fill that gap, both with strong, inspiring mothers who urged us to make a contribution, both attending eastern liberal arts colleges, and so on. Those common experiences don't necessarily provide strength in a relationship between two men—more often the opposite—and we never discussed them. But I think they helped me understand him. My arrival in his life wasn't particularly auspicious, and he was still pretty rough around the edges in his personal style. At several points in the process we thought he was crazy. But *Creating Our Future* is a monument not only to Gordon's intellect but also to his political leadership skills and to his ability to partner. He restored the region's ability to think ahead and the GVRD's ability to be a tool for constructive action."

Resurrecting Regional Planning

THE LIVABLE REGION STRATEGIC PLAN

AND THE GROWTH STRATEGIES ACT

KEN CAMERON WAS eager to present the *Creating Our Future* document to the region's municipal planners in the fall of 1990. He viewed it as the platform for a new era of constructive leadership for the GVRD in many important areas, including air quality, water quality, transportation and growth management. He was initially surprised when the planners' reaction was lukewarm. Part of the explanation was Gordon Campbell's departure from the usual sequence of studious consultation—including consultation with planners—before commitment. But there was a deeper problem, too. "It's a great vision," they told Cameron, "but it's not a plan. It doesn't tell us how we can accommodate the next million people on the ground in a way that reflects the vision." The municipal planners, traditionally wary of any regional oversight that would compromise their autonomy, wanted a regional plan.

Others did too. In a *Vancouver Sun* series later published as a book entitled *From Desolation to Hope*, UBC professors Alan Artibise and Michael Seelig laid out the region's planning challenges in graphic language. Without some overall regional direction with teeth for implementation, they argued, the Lower Mainland was doomed to a future of suburban sprawl and increasing dependence on the private automobile. The development industry had similar concerns. In a move that would be unheard of in most North American cities, the industry's leadership became strong advocates of regional planning as a positive context for community development. This was due in large measure to the broad-minded but savvy leadership of Maureen Enser, the indefatigable executive director of the Urban Development Institute's Pacific Region. She organized a series of seminars and guest speakers on the subject and led the development of the industry's position paper, "Back to the Future," which set out the business case for a new regional plan.

Getting the GVRD back into regional planning was a challenge Cameron saw as both inevitable and dangerous. A year or so earlier, he had been present when Rita Johnston, British Columbia's minister of Municipal Affairs at the time, addressed the annual conference of the Planning Institute of British Columbia. She had outlined some new provisions in the Municipal Act to allow regional districts to provide research and advisory "development services." The new arrangements were a minor step away from the draconian 1983 legislation to eliminate regional planning. Present in the audience was Erik Karlsen, the key architect of the legislation, who recognized that the rump of regional planning remaining at the GVRD would die a slow death without some legislative basis. "These new arrangements will help municipalities to work together on economic development," Johnston intoned, "but they do not bring back regional planning—isn't that right, Erik?" The entire audience of planners answered with a resounding "Yes, Minister!" It may have been the largest collective lie told to a minister by a professional body in British Columbia's history.

Despite the enthusiasm in 1990 of the municipal planners for a regional plan, there was a legal problem. The conventional interpretation of municipal law at the time was "if the Municipal Act doesn't explicitly say you can do it, then you can't do it." There was certainly nothing in the legislation, even with the new provisions Johnston had introduced, that would allow a regional district to prepare a regional growth management plan. And the minister's question for Karlsen showed that the provincial government of the day had no appetite to go back to the future on regional planning.

Cameron took his problem to Gordon Campbell. "The planners say we need a regional plan, which is a good thing, but there's no legislative mandate for it."

"Just start doing it, and see if you can achieve consensus," Campbell replied. "You won't get a mandate for planning now, but you might if you can demonstrate the need for it."

Cameron was incredulous. "You mean that we have to try to put in place a plan that addresses the planning issues of Creating Our Future by consensus?" he asked.

"I mean that in the politics of the GVRD, the only way you can get a plan with relevance to these issues is by consensus," Campbell replied.

Cameron forged ahead. The preparation of what was to become the *Livable Region Strategic Plan* had begun.

GVRD staff started with the basic concepts of Creating Our Future, translating these into a set of criteria that would guide a plan for accommodating the projected population on the region's land base. They seized upon the Creating Our Future concept of a Green Zone as a basic building block for the strategy. After regional and municipal planners had developed criteria, municipalities were asked to nominate lands in their jurisdiction for inclusion in the Green Zone. "This was a very important step," Cameron recalls, "because municipalities have the power to ensure these lands are protected, not only through zoning but also through their ability to form partnerships to acquire lands at risk."

When the municipal proposals were tallied up, the result was amazing. Municipalities had nominated for inclusion in the Green Zone lands amounting to two thirds of the total land area of the Greater Vancouver Regional District. Even excluding the watersheds, mountains and other areas that would never be developed in any case, fully 50 per cent of the developable lowland in this land-short region had been set aside from urbanization by the local government authorities with the ability to make it happen. "It was a double whammy," Cameron recalls. "We had protected the major resource lands in the region, and we had established an urban containment boundary that would force us to be conservative with the land we had left ourselves for the construction of cities and towns. Regions such as Ottawa and Portland had spent years in acrimony attempting to defend green belts and urban growth boundaries that were seen as heavy-handed denial of the development aspirations of landowners and municipalities. Here we had arrived at the same place through a constructive process of consensus."

When the Green Zone proposals were presented to the strategic planning committee, Port Coquitlam Mayor Len Traboulay responded, "The Green Zone is our legacy to future generations." Echoing the Lower Mainland Regional Planning Board's vision of the region as "cities in a sea of green," the creation of the Green Zone solidified a quality that was already making Greater Vancouver different from any other urban region in the world. As it turned out, the Green Zone also became a highly effective tool for urban containment—not its original purpose, but vitally important—in the Livable Region Strategic Plan.

In the discussion at the strategic planning committee, Surrey Mayor Bob Bose, a descendant of a pioneering farm family, described the Green Zone as the working landscape of the region: lands that could include working farms, working forest, resource lands, wetlands and watersheds in addition to open space resources such as parks. "The common feature of lands to be included in the Green Zone," Bose said, "is that they are not to be urbanized. They can have many other uses, but they are set aside from urban development."

Some landowners, notably the owners of Burns Bog, initially expressed concern, but the concept that economic uses other than urbanization would be permitted disarmed their arguments. Also, at that point at least, the Green Zone had no legal impact beyond the local planning and zoning controls already in place, and it could be altered only after due public processes at which the property owner's views would be considered.

GVRD staff then shifted their attention to the policies needed to manage growth within urban areas. These policies essentially deal with changes in where people live, where they work, shop, study and play, and how they travel from one place to another. A provincially led transportation planning process had produced a plan called Freedom to Move, which had been trashed by Vancouver Mayor Gordon Campbell and others as being too road-oriented. The province invited the GVRD to participate in a joint provincial-regional-municipal transportation planning project in the hope that a more acceptable plan could be developed. GVRD Regional Manager Ben Marr agreed to chair a steering committee of provincial and local government officials for the project, and a young transportation economist, Martin Crilly, was hired to lead it.

Cameron saw in these developments an opportunity to do what is often talked about but seldom tried: plan land use and transportation together, interactively. He offered Crilly office space in the GVRD strategic planning department, and he made the department's transportation planning staff available to work virtually full-time on the project, which came to be known as Transport 2021. "*Creating Our Future* said we should put priority on walking, cycling, public transit and goods movement ahead of the private automobile," Cameron recalls. "In that single statement, the region set itself on a different course from any other in North America. To get that kind of transportation system, though, you have to have land use that brings origins and destinations together at sufficient density. With the GVRD also preparing Canada's first air quality management plan, we knew that a key need was to reduce pollution and greenhouse gas emissions by reducing the amount of fuel burned through excessive reliance on private autos."

Meanwhile, another team of GVRD planners was developing scenarios for allocating expected population growth within the region, using the GVRD's unique expertise in demographic analysis and forecasting. The transportation implications of the scenarios were generated by the EMME/2 transportation model, a state-of-the-art interactive transportation planning tool developed at the University of Montreal that could project the demand for additional transportation services from various patterns of land use. The GVRD had acquired the right to develop and use the model within the Greater Vancouver region, making it available for free to local planning staff and their consultants.

There was some huffing and puffing when news of these activities reached the GVRD's critics on municipal councils. Derek Corrigan, elected mayor of Burnaby in 2002, but then a councillor, led the charge over a scenario suggesting that Burnaby accommodate a hundred thousand more people in the next thirty years. Burnaby was fully developed already, Corrigan argued, and had an excellent planning staff. It didn't need any more planning, certainly not from the effete, power-hungry staff at the GVRD. The cause of regional planning was well served, during these and similar discussions, by the patience and political maturity of the other municipal representatives, including Mayor Bob Bose of Surrey, Mayor Gordon Hogg of White Rock, Mayor John Northey of Port Moody and Mayor Marilyn Baker of North Vancouver District. In Burnaby's case, the dialogue revealed that the city strongly favoured protecting the Agricultural Land Reserve. But the ALR would be put under severe pressure if growth sprawled up the Fraser Valley because it could not be accommodated in Burnaby and other more central cities. It was pointed out to Corrigan that many of the people in those developments would have jobs in Burnaby and Vancouver, with travel by automobile through Burnaby's streets their only transportation alternative. Then there was the city's growing aspiration for redevelopment along the Broadway-Lougheed corridor, with high-density centres at the Brentwood and Lougheed malls and a new rapid transit line as a catalyst. "Gradually, with the consistent support for a regional perspective by the Burnaby planning staff, the City of Burnaby became a supporter of accommodating additional growth," Ken Cameron says. "Today, Mayor Corrigan is one of the Livable Region Strategic Plan's strongest advocates."

"In the preparation of the regional growth management plan, each municipality went through a similar thought process, either in dialogue with their colleagues and us or on their own," Cameron remembers. "Each ultimately reached the conclusion that their aspirations and the region's best interests could be complementary. The self-imposed discipline of reconciling each municipality's growth numbers with the regional totals created a basis for negotiation and dialogue."

By early 1992, the various growth management concepts were ready to be tested with the public. "Getting public input at a regional level is a significant challenge," Cameron notes. "It's hard to have a dialogue with a couple of million people." The method selected was two large day-long conferences. At the first conference, in May 1992, the guest speaker was Mike Harcourt, British Columbia's newly elected NDP premier, who committed his support to regional planning and collaboration. The second conference was held in November of that year, with the express direction from the strategic planning committee to narrow the focus from several possible growth management concepts to one. Cameron recognized that small-group discussions at conferences are necessary to build understanding and permit more informed choices, but he wanted to override the tendency for such groups to be dominated by the opinions of one or two people who usually got themselves designated as spokespersons. Above all, he wanted to avoid the tedious "reporting back" process that can deaden the momentum generated by group discussions. "To me," Cameron says, "there are only two legitimate entities at a meeting: the individual and the group as a whole. So we devised a system of balloting that could be tallied on the spot. When the technology to do this failed at the last moment, Judy Kirk and her consultant, Andrew Mackie, recruited some students to add up the results by hand."

The result was a move over the course of the day towards the "Compact Metropolitan Area" scenario, leaving out of further consideration the "Current

Trends" (more aptly seen as "Sprawl Up the Valley") and "North of the River" scenarios. "By the end of the conference," Cameron says, "the strategic planning committee's objective had been met. The basic growth management concept for the region was established, although we all noted that there was some support developing for 'None of the Above.' It was time to quit while we were ahead."

As the plan took shape, the need arose for an adoption process and for clarification of the plan's effect on municipalities and others. Working with Mayor Gordon Hogg and some municipal staff, Cameron developed a procedure that could be incorporated into a GVRD board resolution. The proposed plan would be formally circulated to municipalities to give them an opportunity to lodge objections; if objections were received, the timetable for adoption would be extended to permit their resolution. Any objections outstanding at the end of the specified period would simply be noted in the plan, which would require a 75 per cent majority of the board for approval. The plan would have no effect on any party without that party's agreement. "Without provincial legislation, our plan could have no teeth," Cameron says. "That underscored the importance of reaching consensus, which we defined as 'the absence of expressed dissent.' "

The emerging Transport 2021 plan and its interdependence with the regional land use plan drew the process into the highest-stakes intermunicipal game of

them all: competition for new rapid transit lines link-
ing the regional town centres and Vancouver's downtown. When the Transport 2021 Medium Range Plan
proposed three new light rail lines by 2006, the game
was on. The two potential purposes of a rapid transit
investment are to "shape" growth by providing supe-
rior access to the places targeted for high density, or
to "serve" demand by building transit where it can
attract the most riders. From the "shape" perspective,
a line extending from New Westminster to Coquitlam
Regional Town Centre was the most beneficial choice.
From the perspective of "serving" demand, the most
attractive option was a line from downtown Vancouver
to Richmond. In championing a third line, from Broadway and Granville to the Lougheed Mall, Burnaby suggested that both effects could be achieved.

A 1993 study comparing the three lines, completed
by Marvin Shaffer for B.C. Transit, shed some significant light on the question. Shaffer concluded that
building new light rail transit could not be justified
economically if the sole objective was to serve existing demand and attract new riders; there were cheaper
ways to achieve this objective. That appeared to rule
out the Richmond line. The only justifiable reason for
building new rail facilities, the study said, would be to
shape growth in a more desirable direction. The report
went on, however, to predict that the New Westminster
to Coquitlam line would have very low ridership and
require a very high subsidy. The Broadway-Lougheed

line would have more moderate growth-shaping influence but better operational economics. The release of the report was an indication that the Broadway-Lougheed line enjoyed substantial support within the provincial government.

The rail transit issue had a significant influence on the most contentious aspect of the growth management planning process: growth allocations. The initial set of allocations prepared by GVRD planning staff, based on principles derived from *Creating Our Future* and other documents, turned out to be so radically different from the political aspirations of the municipalities that they were referred back to staff for revision. For Ken Cameron, this was very frustrating. He remembers, "When David Marsh, a reporter with the Surrey *Leader,* asked me what we were going to do about this, I said the planning staff were going to go to the top of our head office building, hold hands and jump. I was only half sorry when I realized I was on the record and the quote would appear in the paper." However, the response of the municipalities was tempered by their desire to show that they could accommodate the growth and density required to win their particular transit line. The GVRD staff presented revised growth allocations that, though more influenced by trends and ambition than the original numbers had been, reflected a significant move in the direction set by the planning principles and the "Compact Metropolitan Area" scenario.

The rail transit issue also eased approval of the Transport 2021 Medium and Long Range Plans. "With the political minds so focussed on rapid transit, the other potentially controversial components of those plans, including transportation demand management and bridge tolling, went through without a whimper," Cameron recalls. The GVRD board pulled out the transit phasing issue from the remainder of the plans in an attempt to reach consensus on it. The result was a motion affirming that all three lines were needed in the medium term, but priority should go to building the Broadway-Lougheed and Coquitlam–New Westminster lines as a single system, later dubbed the "T" line. Richmond was outraged. They did not know then that their city would have the last laugh.

In the meantime, wheels were turning behind the scenes. Derek Corrigan, at this point chair of B.C. Transit, and the minister responsible for transit, Glen Clark, were quietly lining up approval for the "L" line, which would connect Broadway to Lougheed and then to Coquitlam, leaving the section connecting to New Westminster for a later time. "It made no sense from a transportation perspective," Cameron recalls, "but it appeared that Vancouver was prepared to vote for it. If that happened, then all hell would break loose."

When an announcement by the province appeared to be imminent, Surrey Mayor Bob Bose, as chair of the strategic planning committee, arranged a meeting for committee members with Premier Mike Harcourt and Municipal Affairs Minister Darlene Marzari. The GVRD representatives stated bluntly that the implementation of the "L line" would deeply divide the region.

"What are you going to do?" demanded Greg Halsey-Brandt, mayor of Richmond and chair of the GVRD board.

"I'm going to cancel the announcement," Harcourt replied. "Glen and Derek assured me that this announcement would be welcomed in the region. If that's not the case, then it won't happen."

A few weeks later, reporters called to a press conference in Burnaby for a major transportation announcement were puzzled to find the premier announcing only a few minor highway improvements. The GVRD had been given a little more time to try to heal its house divided.

"It was such a classic demonstration of the differences between Mike Harcourt and Glen Clark as politicians," Darlene Marzari would later observe. "If you wanted to sell something to Mike, you had to say that both sides would win. If you wanted to sell something to Glen, you had to say that we would win and the other side would lose."

In late 1994, the draft of what was now called the *Livable Region Strategic Plan* was approved in principle by the GVRD board, with so little debate and fanfare that councillor Gordon Price felt compelled to bring the board's attention to the historic nature of the moment. As agreed, the plan would now be circulated to member municipalities for formal approval. "The consensus process is like ironing a shirt," is how Cameron puts it today. "At first it looks like an impossible task, but if you go at it thoroughly and perhaps go over some areas twice or three times, eventually you have something wearable."

Darlene Marzari, for her part, had begun to address the NDP's long-standing interest in restoring regional planning. Shortly after her appointment as Municipal Affairs minister, she and Cameron found themselves on the same Helijet flight from Victoria to Vancouver.

"I want to talk to you," she said, "but I have a staff and you have a board. How can we get together?"

Cameron suggested a briefing on the Livable Region Strategic Plan, and a few days later he gave his PowerPoint presentation to an audience of one in the minister's constituency office. Through endless presentations and discussions, GVRD staff had boiled the plan's essence down to four propositions totalling fifteen words:

· Protect the Green Zone.

· Build complete communities.

· Achieve a compact metropolitan region.

· Increase transportation choice.

THE MINISTER EXPRESSED her support for the plan immediately, and she asked Cameron to serve on a working group to prepare new growth management legislation for the province.

"It was a tremendous privilege to serve on that group," recalls Cameron, "as well as an opportunity for which regional planners had waited for more than ten years." Even more important, the work provided a chance both to legitimize the Livable Region Strategic Plan and to create the legislative mandate that had been missing when the plan first got underway. When the Growth Strategies Act was passed in June 1995, it reflected the non-hierarchical, consensus-based approach to planning that the GVRD had been following. It also included provisions that permitted the minister to deem plans that were in preparation prior to June 1995 to be regional growth strategies under the legislation. In gaining the formal support of member municipalities and in other activities leading up to the Livable Region Strategic Plan's adoption, GVRD staff were careful to follow (and to document that they had followed) the requirements of the emerging act.

By September 1995, there were three municipalities that had declined to support the Livable Region Strategic Plan: the Township of Langley, the City of Surrey and the City of Richmond. GVRD staff continued negotiations with these municipalities into the fall, reaching agreements in the form of memoranda of understanding with both Langley and Surrey in

October. These memoranda, frequently misinterpreted as exempting those municipalities from the plan, simply acknowledged certain municipal aspirations in return for the municipalities' agreement to support the adoption of the plan. The memorandum with Surrey has been the more misunderstood of the two. "In reality," Cameron explains, "it stated that the city would support adoption of the plan and that the region would not expect or ask the City of Surrey to reverse or alter planning and zoning decisions it had already made. That was easy; the Livable Region Strategic Plan was always about future planning decisions, and about shaping those decisions in a different direction over the longer term. It's too bad that some Surrey councillors later chose to forget that their city's formal support for the plan was part of the deal."

The agreements with Surrey and Langley Township left Richmond still angling for a rapid transit line. That city's objection was based on the fact that the western part of Lulu Island, its city centre, was not included in the Growth Concentration Area and consequently (the city feared) could be assigned a lower priority for rapid transit. GVRD staff had excluded the area through the application of one of the first principles of planning: that additional settlement should not be located in areas subject to natural hazards—in this case flooding and potential liquefaction of soils in the event of an earthquake—if there are acceptable alternatives.

Cameron and his staff knew this was a moment of truth, morally and professionally. The plan's provisions gave Richmond almost everything the city could want. They supported Richmond as a regional town centre; included the Richmond rapid transit line as an early priority; supported continued employment growth in Richmond, including the expansion of Vancouver International Airport; and even continued population growth up to the limit set in the city's current Official Community Plan. The only thing the plan did not support was residential development beyond that limit.

As the issue heated up, Richmond city council committed a blunder of epic proportions by asking that the dispute be resolved through the provisions of the new Growth Strategies Act. These provisions called for mediation through the minister of Municipal Affairs, leading to binding arbitration if mediation was unsuccessful. An awkward aspect of the situation was the fact that Richmond Mayor Greg Halsey-Brandt was also chair of the GVRD. On at least one occasion, he had found himself signing letters from himself as mayor to himself as chair.

The escalation of the dispute led, on Cameron's part, to further examination of the implications for both sides of winning or losing at arbitration. The provincial ministry of Environment, Lands and Parks had confirmed that the flood hazard was real, and the ministry had been pressuring the City of Richmond to improve flood protection. If the GVRD lost, the Livable Region Strategic Plan would be altered to include the western part of Lulu Island in the Growth Concentration Area—not a good thing, but in practical terms not the end of the world. If Richmond lost, the city would have the flood hazard confirmed publicly and could well be compelled to undertake expensive additional flood protection works, including a new dike across the middle of Lulu Island that would cut the city in half and cost about $20 million.

"Okay," Cameron thought as he reviewed the file, "let her rip."

Some of the same thinking may have been going on at Richmond City Hall. Media coverage of the flood hazard had also been picked up on by some important overseas property owners and potential investors. In any event, Minister Marzari had little difficulty setting up a mediation meeting with the two parties represented by Halsey-Brandt as required by the act and even less difficulty in persuading the mayor/chair to instruct Richmond and GVRD staff to sort the mess out. A power lunch between Ken Cameron and Richmond City Manager Johnny Carline produced a memorandum of understanding that was quickly approved by both sides. Greater Vancouver now had a regional plan that was formally supported by all twenty-one municipalities, and British Columbia's Growth Strategies Act had produced closure in a dispute for the first time.

All that remained were the formalities. Premier Mike Harcourt attended a Council of Councils meeting at the Vancouver Trade and Convention Centre on February 10, 1996, where he and the assembled hundred or so municipal councillors were witnesses as Darlene Marzari signed an order under the Growth Strategies Act deeming the Livable Region Strategic Plan to be a regional growth strategy. "I remember the occasion well," says Harcourt today. "It was one of my last official acts as premier."

As easy as ironing a shirt.

The Greater Vancouver Transportation Authority

GEORGE PUIL MAKES

A DEAL WITH THE DEVIL

WHEN COUNCILLOR GEORGE Puil of Vancouver landed unexpectedly in the chairperson's seat at the Greater Vancouver Regional District board meeting on December 6, 1996, his first words were, "I want to do something about transportation in this region."

The vacancy had been created only a few days earlier when Richmond city council declined to re-elect the current chair, Mayor Greg Halsey-Brandt, to the GVRD board. Halsey-Brandt had been trying to line up support among the board members for another one-year term as chair, but the Richmond council decision brought an abrupt end to his career in regional politics.

"GVRD Vice-Chair Mark Sager actually encouraged me to run for the chair of the GVRD after he decided not to run for re-election as mayor of West Vancouver, and Gordon Campbell [by then leader of the B.C.

Liberals] also encouraged me," Puil recalls. "When Halsey-Brandt found out that I was going to run, he had his executive assistant call me and say that he wanted it for one more year. Would I not run and he would back me the following year? But I had fully intended to contest the position even if he had been appointed to the board, as I knew I had the backing of a majority of the board."

Puil had served on Vancouver city council and on the GVRD board for many years, specializing in financial issues and chairing the GVRD's solid waste committee. Although he had gained the respect of the elected people and staff who worked with him directly, among the broader regional community his reputation was as a scrappy, partisan, take-no-prisoners loner who had survived by applying the tactics of his successful rugby career to the political arena. When rumours of his candidacy began to circulate, some GVRD staffers had trouble suppressing their anxiety about this impending change in leadership.

Delta Mayor Beth Johnson was elected vice-chair of the GVRD board, and Puil also appointed her as chair of the Strategic Planning Committee, enlisting a powerful ally and nicely balancing the issues of gender and geography.

In politics, timing is nearly everything, and what isn't timing is optics.

The main impetus for Puil's selection of transportation as his priority was a poll indicating that transportation was a major public concern. At the time, he was only vaguely aware of machinery working away at the staff level that would give him an opportunity to acquire the control over transportation that had eluded local government for decades. The origin of the staff work lay in the vexatious dispute over phasing of the three light rapid transit lines called for by 2006 in the Transport 2021 Medium Range Plan. After much dissension, the GVRD board had voted in 1994 to give priority to the "T" line, comprising the Broadway-Lougheed and Coquitlam–New Westminster lines, which the board wished to see constructed as a single project, with whatever phasing in of service was most efficient from the perspectives of both transportation and construction.

The provincial government, now led by Premier Glen Clark after Mike Harcourt's resignation in early 1996, was receptive to the GVRD board's recommendation but pointed out that there was insufficient funding to build the "T" line all at once. GVRD representatives were open to a creative solution to this problem, as long as it didn't involve using property taxes to pay for transit. GVRD staff began negotiating with provincial staff a protocol agreement for the planning, design and construction of the rapid transit line. Some provincial requirements were ironic in the context of later developments, par-ticularly the province's insistence on considering only conventional at-grade light rail transit technology. That was an attempt, ultimately unsuccessful, to wean the region from the sole-supplier, capital-intensive Sky-Train technology.

As discussions continued, GVRD staff made the point that if locally generated funds were to be used in the project, there should be some change in governance from the provincially dominated B.C. Transit structure. It also became clear that the governance of rapid transit could not really be separated from the governance of the rest of the transit system. Consequently, a decision was made to split the protocol agreement into two agreements: one for negotiating the construction of the "T" rapid transit line and a separate agreement (soon dubbed the "G and F agreement") for negotiating new governance and funding arrangements for transportation.

The "T" line rapid transit agreement did not run far before it hit a brick wall. The agreement called for a steering committee representing the municipalities affected to appoint a project director from a list prepared by the province. "We knew something was up when the provincial people asked what would happen if the list only contained one name," Ken Cameron recalls. "Game over, we replied." So it was that the rapid transit project reverted to a conventional provincial project rather than the co-operative effort that had been contemplated. The prime qualification of the project director that the province selected was that she be able to get something—anything—built before the next provincial election. The result was the Millennium "Line," not a line at all but fragments of two lines that connected the New Westminster hub of the existing line back to itself at Broadway and Commercial Drive. The two lines ran within waving distance of each other at that location, leading one wag to label the area "Active Pass," after the narrow passage in which the B.C. Ferries pass each other en route between the Lower Mainland, the Gulf Islands and Vancouver Island. The line made no sense in transportation terms, and it didn't help in political terms, either; as the result of an unrelated scandal, Clark's NDP was reduced to two seats in the 2001 election.

The "G and F agreement" was moving along, however, assisted by three serendipitous developments. The first was the appointment of Clive Rock, a former B.C. Transit executive, to head the GVRD's transportation planning staff. Because of his long-standing friendship with Rock, Ken Cameron approached the hiring process for the vacancy within the strategic planning department with scrupulous objectivity, including the use of a selection committee whose membership included regional manager Ben Marr and some municipal types. "Clive has the best strategic transportation planning mind in Canada," Cameron says. "I told him that the selection committee had recommended his appointment, but that I wanted him to be careful not to be a pain in the ass, because I was familiar with his abilities in that area also." The second key development was the Ministry of Transportation and Highways' appointment of John Mills, another B.C. Transit refugee and a good friend of both Cameron and Rock, as manager of planning for the South Coast region. The third development was the abrupt and unilateral decision the Clark government had made to download to municipalities the responsibility for provincial secondary highways, which essentially functioned as part of the arterial road system in many parts of the region. These three events created an opportunity for the GVRD to include in the "G and F" negotiations new arrangements for the governance and funding of the major roads of regional significance in Greater Vancouver. An unwelcome downloading move turned into a golden opportunity to design a new governance and funding system for both roads and transit.

The protocol agreement called for both the GVRD and the province to appoint negotiators. Both sides had their eye on Marvin Shaffer, who had conducted the study of the three transit lines for the province and had worked on solid waste issues for the GVRD. "He was a talented policy analyst who had a lot of credibility with the province," Cameron says, "but we got him first." Partly as a result of having their prime candidate snaffled by the other side, the province took a few months to select as their negotiators Bob Lingwood, a

B.C. Transit executive, and Peter Cameron (no relation to Ken), a labour relations specialist. It was clear that the government was wary of the notoriously militant and unpredictable transit union.

The GVRD board used this period to define its objectives for the negotiations. It wanted to move forward on transportation on a broad and strategic level. It was prepared to use some of its existing tax revenue sources to buy a role for the region in transportation, while pursuing new transportation revenue sources, and it was willing to help develop proposals for major changes in governance if the province and the municipalities had an appetite for this. In the fall of 1996, Ken Cameron made the rounds with the twenty-one member councils to explain the board's objectives and the protocol agreements (there were still two at that point) and to get input.

Finally the province was willing to sign the agreement for negotiations. The minister responsible for transit, Joy McPhail, attended a Council of Councils meeting at the Burnaby Firefighters' Hall on April 7, 1997, for a signing ceremony with Puil. "The suspicion and hostility in the room were palpable," Cameron recalls. "The municipalities didn't trust the GVRD, and nobody trusted the province. Everybody thought everybody else had a hidden agenda. There couldn't be two more opposite people than Joy McPhail and George Puil—in political persuasion, gender, age, you name it." Many were skeptical that Puil could lead this process or sell the results to the municipalities. "Yet you never know," mused Gordon Price, a fellow Vancouver councillor and GVRD director at the time, in a conversation with Ken Cameron. "It could be a case of Nixon to China."

A workshop held at Vancouver's Robson Square in May 1997 provided the first opportunity to test the views of a new crop of actors on the regional board, including Doug McCallum, who had defeated Bob Bose to become the new mayor of Surrey. Board members seemed to be on side with pursuing the goals of the Livable Region Strategic Plan/Transport 2021 by bringing transit under local control, making the road download workable and implementing transportation demand management, all within a stable and predictable financial framework. It was on the question of whether this should be a job for the GVRD or for a new entity that rationality appeared to evaporate. It was clear any proposal that appeared to add power to the GVRD would be in for a rough ride. "Optics again," Cameron observes today.

The negotiators had a little more than six months— until October 31, 1997—to come up with an agreement for consideration by the parties and possible ratification by member municipalities. Cameron gives Shaffer most of the credit for the extraordinary agreement that resulted. "Marvin had worked successfully on sensitive projects with both sides and enjoyed their confidence. He believed there was no public policy problem that would not ultimately succumb to rigorous and comprehensive analysis. He realized that creating new arrangements for transportation was essential to enable the parties to get on with their respective policy agendas—debt reduction and disentanglement for the province and local control to implement the regional plan for the GVRD."

The model guiding the GVRD staff's thinking was the various "districts" that had been created over the years for water supply, sewerage and drainage, etc. Each of these embodied the concepts of membership by municipalities, a governing board that included representatives from all members, agreed-upon service areas, and utility-type revenue sources appropriate to the services being provided. Not surprisingly, the provincial negotiators had in mind the existing model of a provincial crown corporation, B.C. Transit, supplemented by regional transit commissions in the Vancouver and Victoria regions comprising area mayors appointed by the province in accordance with a formula for area representation. They regarded the GVRD board as too large and unwieldy to be the governance body for transportation, and although they ultimately agreed in the negotiations that the GVRD board should appoint the local government representatives to the transportation board, they insisted on retaining a formula for area representation and on having three provincial seats on the board.

The existing regional transit commission concept was dismissed by the Vancouver Regional Transit Commission's own members, who felt they received all the complaints but had little power to respond to them. Len Traboulay, Port Coquitlam mayor and long-term Vancouver Regional Transit Commission chair, described the role acerbically in a comment to the GVRD strategic planning committee: "We're just flak catchers for the provincial government."

As the negotiations got underway, the idea of a new transportation "district" affiliated with the GVRD was recognized as a political non-starter, with no support from the province and very mixed views from the local government side. Discussions then began to address what a new entity might look like—its responsibilities, powers and financing. "Everything was hypothetical at that stage, because we knew any solution would have to be not only workable but saleable in the wacky world of GVRD politics," Cameron recalls.

The responsibilities of the new entity were fairly easy to identify. It would have all the functions of B.C. Transit within the "transportation service area" (the GVRD). It would have the ability to designate a "Major Road Network" and provide funding to municipalities for that network's capital improvement, operations and maintenance. It would provide transportation demand management programs to encourage residents to select the most efficient modes and times of travel.

Although the decision to move the GVRD planning department's transportation planning responsibilities and staff to the new body had a certain logic, it was a tough one for Ken Cameron to swallow. "It was ironic. The very thing that had produced an innovative, integrated regional plan for land use and transportation was the existence of two teams working together in a co-management structure. Now that would be rent asunder. The two teams would not only be in different management structures—they would be reporting to different political entities." His concerns were partially assuaged by a provision that the transportation entity would be required to deliver its services in accordance with the Livable Region Strategic Plan/Transport 2021 and in support of the region's air quality objectives and economic development. To give the new body a delivery role in air quality, it would be assigned the responsibility within Greater Vancouver for AirCare, the provincial vehicle emission testing system.

A key innovation was that the new body would be given the power to deliver its services in a variety of ways—directly, through subsidiaries it could create, or through contracts with municipalities or private parties. This not only recognized existing arrangements such as the municipally operated West Vancouver transit system, but it created flexibility for delivery of new services that would permit the restructuring of the monolithic B.C. Transit organization, which had operated and maintained the region's mainstream bus fleet for more than fifteen years.

Not unexpectedly, the financial elements of the new arrangements posed the greatest challenges for the negotiators and their principals. The province wanted to get rid of some debt and to cap or reduce their annual contribution of about $250 million to transit in Greater Vancouver; it considered transit to be a local service that should be supported by local taxes, particularly the property tax. Provincial representatives pointed out that Greater Vancouver was the only metropolitan area in Canada where transit was not funded by property taxes. The GVRD wanted to maintain the provincial contribution, to have a tamper-proof set of financial arrangements, to avoid the use of the property tax and to implement the utility principle that transportation services should be paid for by transportation users, namely transit riders and road users.

Fortunately, the financial arrangements that existed at the time offered some fertile ground for reconciling these positions. The GVRD had a hospital capital planning and financing function that raised about $50 million per year through property taxes, an amount so small in relation to the provincial share of hospital financing that the GVRD's role in approvals

had been described as a "speed bump" for most decisions. If the province were to assume the cost of all
hospital capital spending in the region, the property
tax "room" could be used to support transportation
without any impact on the taxpayer.

"That was a hard one for me to accept," George Puil
recalls. "We had been so vehemently opposed to using
the property tax for transit, and Premier Clark was
booed at a Union of British Columbia Municipalities
convention for fooling around with property taxes, so
there was no trust. Few of us believed that it would
stay at $50 million, and history has proven us right.
I'm still not sure we made the right decision."

On the user-pay side, there was fertile ground
too. Transit fares would be available to the new entity.
Although provincial treasury staff have traditionally
been opposed to allocating the provincial fuel taxes
on a regional basis as a road-user charge, an earlier
administration had implemented a gasoline surtax
of four cents per litre in the region to support transit. This precedent, combined with the logic of fuel
tax paying for transportation, including roads in the
Major Road Network, proved irresistible. A formula for
gradually transferring an additional two cents over six
years was developed, permitting the revenue impact to
be absorbed by the province. This seemed a good way
to continue the provincial contribution, at least in
part. Although everyone recognized that the province

could change the implementing legislation at any time, by this point in the negotiations George Puil had had a number of private meetings with Joy McPhail, who was also minister of Finance, and he was feeling more comfortable. "I actually began to like her," he recalls.

The user-pay principle was also reflected in provisions that would enable the transportation agency to bring in an annual levy on vehicles registered in the region, tolls on facilities it owned and a tax on parking spaces.

The $1.5 billion debt attached to the initial SkyTrain represented a further opportunity to meet the objectives of each side creatively. The province had required the transit system to make payments on this debt from the beginning; they were a financial millstone not of transit's making that had seriously impeded a badly needed expansion of the region's bus system. During negotiations, it was agreed that the province would retain responsibility for $1 billion of that debt and transfer $500 million to the new entity.

As the October 31, 1997, deadline for an agreement approached, the negotiators and their principals began to see a good chance of a successful conclusion. Recognizing that the new organization's birthday would be Halloween, they decided to stop referring to it as the "Entity" and selected the "Greater Vancouver Transportation Authority (GVTA)" instead. (It would later rename itself "TransLink." "Too clever by half," Cameron still grumbles.)

The negotiators had a final marathon round at Marvin Shaffer's office in White Rock on Saturday, October 25, keeping GVRD staff up to date by phone. As darkness fell, they inked the agreement and then went out for a celebratory dinner. The next day, GVRD senior staff, including Chief Administrative Officer Johnny Carline, Ken Cameron and Clive Rock, assembled in Cameron's office to copy the agreement for distribution to the GVRD board's oversight committee. That afternoon they fanned out to deliver the package to the committee members at home. "Will it fly?" they wondered.

The oversight committee, chaired by Mayor Beth Johnson of Delta, had been engaged enough in the issues as negotiations proceeded to absorb the magnitude and the promise of the deal. The committee included among its members Vancouver councillor Gordon Price and Burnaby councillor Lee Rankin, both people with intelligence and experience with planning and financial matters.

The same could not be said for the broader audience of local government politicians. Many of them saw the agreement as a deal with the devil and a stalking horse for the further pillage of local authorities by the Glen Clark government. A six-month period ending February 28, 1998, was set out in the negotiators' agreement for reaching ratification by the province and the GVRD. This would be a significant challenge, given the complexity of the agreement, the low levels of trust many harboured with respect to both the GVRD and the province, and the need for the GVRD board to have solid support from member municipalities for a decision of this magnitude.

The first priority in establishing credibility for the recommended agreement was to undertake two due-diligence initiatives. Clive Rock and Ian Jarvis, GVRD treasurer, collaborated on a financial analysis and forecast that confirmed that the new authority would have sufficient revenues to meet a level of transportation investment consistent with the goals of the Livable Region Strategic Plan/Transport 2021. An engineering firm from Calgary was retained to do a video "condition assessment" of the roads that would become part of the Major Road Network.

The next step was a communications plan to explain the agreement. Under the energetic leadership of Robert Paddon, the GVRD's newly appointed manager of communications and education, a tabloid print summary was prepared on both the agreement and the process for its review prior to ratification, and a series of public meetings was organized around the region.

Recognizing the importance of personal communication in winning over the municipal councils, and inspired by Gordon Campbell's road trip to sell Creating Our Future, George Puil led a round of meetings with them. Nearly every Monday night for several months running, Cameron and Rock would pick Puil up at home for a nocturnal journey aimed at selling the deal. In the midst of all this, Puil had to have surgery to replace one of his rugby-wrecked knees. This left him in considerable pain and unable to stand for long periods of time. "It didn't do much for his patience, either," Cameron recalls.

The West Vancouver municipal council was one of the most vociferously suspicious of the proposed agreement. Led by two councillors who were former Social Credit cabinet members and assisted by a rookie councillor from the land development sector, the council saw the deal in entirely partisan terms, despite Mayor Pat Boname's attempts to be rational. Puil's encounter with the council would be critical, especially since it was to be carried live on the North Shore cable network.

"They kept George on his feet at the lectern for the better part of an hour," Cameron recalls. "They could see how much pain he was in, but they were so blinded by political rage at a government they thought George had somehow come to represent that they wouldn't even offer him a chance to sit in a chair and answer their questions. I remember thinking that I had often seen mental torture in municipal politics, but never physical torture. But George took everything they threw at him and was literally still standing at the end. The man had enough guts to match his conviction that this was the right thing to do."

The meetings with the other councils were more civil but heavily dominated by local agendas in transportation. The deal had to have something in it for everyone. "Fortunately," Cameron recalls, "due to the inclusion of road funding in the agreement, there *was* something in it for everyone—or there could be with a little tweaking—and the benefits to the region as a whole were substantial."

The public meetings were charged with suspicion and fear that the province and the GVRD were conspiring in a new attack on the taxpayers. One commentator, a retired Concorde pilot, got great mileage out of the simple fact that the "socialist" NDP government was involved. It was an odd perspective coming from someone who had spent a lifetime in one of the most subsidized transportation projects in history. Others advanced outlandish hypotheses to challenge the financial aspects of the deal. "What if people stopped driving their cars? What would *that* do to your fuel tax revenues?"

The region-wide controversy spilled over into the media. Elizabeth Aird, in her "Urban Scrawl" column in the *Vancouver Sun*, ridiculed the dissenters. "They can't take 'yes' for an answer," she wrote. "If Doug McCallum and his cohorts succeed in deep-sixing this deal, they deserve a special place in hell where they wait forever, in the rain, for a B.C. Transit bus that never comes." The underlying reality was that the negotiators' agreement was standing up very well to questions, at least those based upon reasonable probabilities.

The consultation came to a head in a Council of Councils meeting at the Inn at Westminster Quay on January 31, 1998. The room was crowded; the atmosphere was charged with suspicion only partially offset by the enthusiasm of the many councillors who had concluded that the agreement represented the chance of a political lifetime. The West Vancouver contingent was braying in full chorus, with one of them calling Johnny Carline "the most dangerous man in the region."

The positive results of the due-diligence studies on finances and the condition of the roads were to be presented, but the GVRD staff had a dirty little secret. The study of the roads had failed to take account of the fact that some roads were two-lane and some were four-lane. Since all were in good condition, this overlooked detail didn't make any difference to the validity of the study, but the Calgary-based consultant felt it would be important to point out this error in his presentation. Ken Cameron realized that any confession of error, no matter how immaterial, would be seized upon to destroy the study's credibility. It was forcefully suggested to the consultant that he not mention this little problem. After his presentation, the consultant expressed an interest in lingering on and mingling with the crowd. Instead, Cameron packed him into a taxi with instructions to the driver to take him straight to the airport.

One of the most perplexing reactions to the proposed agreement was the reluctance of some councils to participate in the establishment of the Major Road Network, which involved no loss of control by the municipality but did render them eligible for funding for operations, maintenance and, potentially, capital projects. "They seem to be saying, 'We'll show you,'" Clive Rock observed at the time. "'We won't take your money. You'll be sorry!'"

As the GVRD staff report recommending ratification wended its way through the GVRD committee structure in February, it was obvious that the agreement enjoyed a significant level of support. But there was to be one last hurdle to clear. An individual by the name of Sam Ahad applied to the B.C. Supreme Court for an injunction to prevent the GVRD board from voting on the agreement, on the grounds that the GVRD had said in its publication that the public would be consulted and, in Ahad's view, such consultation had not occurred. GVRD staff were perplexed. No one could figure out whom, if anyone, Ahad represented, and why he had launched this challenge. "It's still a mystery," Cameron says today. Although it was almost inconceivable that a court would accept this argument and interfere with an elected body's right to make a decision, the matter had to be taken seriously. The GVRD's high-priced legal counsel was briefed on the case, and the motion was heard just two days before the board was scheduled to vote. The judge's decision, handed down the night before the board meeting, not only dismissed but demolished the case put forward by Ahad and awarded costs to the GVRD. "I considered it my sacred duty to ensure that every penny owed to the GVRD was collected," Cameron recalls.

The debate on ratification of the agreement at the GVRD board meeting on February 27, 1998, was lengthy and raucous, but it passed by a majority of 70 per cent. After the meeting, Ken Cameron held a party in his MetroTower II office to celebrate. He and Rock presented Puil and Johnson with army flak jackets with the words "GVTA Flak Catcher" emblazoned on them. "The reason we were successful was that there was real teamwork between politicians and staff," Cameron recalls. "We wanted to recognize that."

Shortly afterwards, the province also ratified the agreement and began drafting the legislation necessary to implement it. The legislation was introduced in June 1998 and passed in July, and the Greater Vancouver Transportation Authority opened its doors on April 1, 1999—two years less a week from the commencement of negotiations. "In comparison with most government initiatives, the GVTA was set up in the blink of an eye," Cameron says today. Few noticed that the entity conceived in a process ending on Halloween was born on April Fools' Day.

Almost immediately the GVTA began to attract international attention for its innovative features, including putting roads, transit and transportation demand management under one political roof; requiring that transportation and land use plans reinforce each other; and using transportation revenues to pay for transportation services. Cameron and Rock developed a tag-team presentation on the new arrangements for audiences in other parts of Canada, in Europe and in China.

One of the early visitors to research the new arrangements was the junior minister for Transportation from the United Kingdom, the former actress Glenda Jackson. Puil had a lengthy meeting with the minister. A few days later, he was addressing an audience of construction executives about the GVTA, and he mentioned his meeting with Jackson. "Then a couple of nights later I turned on the TV and—Jesus Christ—there she was in *Sons and Lovers*—nude!"

Puil would go on to become the chair of the GVTA, in addition to his role as chair of the GVRD, and to endure horrible conflicts over the aborted introduction of a vehicle levy and a three-month transit strike in which a load of horse manure was dumped on his front lawn. His ultimate defeat as a Vancouver city councillor in the elections of November 2002 was widely attributed to his role as chair of the GVTA. He was succeeded by Doug McCallum, who somewhere along the way had convinced himself that the organization had value after all. McCallum was defeated as mayor of Surrey while playing this role, creating the reputation of the GVTA chair's position as the political death seat of the region.

"I always thought a regional organization that tried to fix Greater Vancouver's transportation problems would have a challenging task, and I wasn't wrong," Cameron says now. "But I still regard the GVTA as a thing of rare beauty in its concept and scope. The region is much better off today than it would have been without the process of change that George Puil led."

Power Shift

THE PROVINCE'S ROLE

ERRY MCGEER, VANCOUVER'S Depression-era
mayor, was a man who knew a thing or two about
the limits of intergovernmental co-operation. He
served not only as Vancouver's twenty-third and
twenty-seventh mayors but also—often simulta-
neously with his civic duties—as a member of British Columbia's legislature and of both the House of
Commons and the Senate. McGeer's political career
remains unique in Canadian electoral history. It often
made him a deliverer of bad news from afar. He became
famous in April 1934 for reading the Riot Act to relief
camp workers, many of them World War I veterans, at
Vancouver's Victory Square cenotaph.

"You see," he told the men, "we have bullets for you
but we haven't bread." McGeer felt that Ottawa's cal-
lous indifference was a symptom of the sheer distance

from Vancouver to the nation's capital. Twenty-five hundred miles eastbound is a long way, McGeer noted, "but it is ten times as far from Ottawa to Vancouver."

McGeer made that observation upon being elevated to the Senate in 1945. Often, though, as he well knew, the distance from Vancouver to Ottawa is less a journey into another reality than is the ninety-minute voyage from Vancouver to Victoria. As we so often hear it said, every city, town and regional district in B.C. is "a creature of the province." The word evokes the image of a small, furry animal without much say in the overall scheme of things. How does that square with our new understanding of the wealth-generating role of cities? Especially information technology-based economies like Greater Vancouver's, in which processing industrial raw materials plays a lesser role than it used to?

Actually, every Canadian city is a creature of its provincial government. This arrangement was decreed 157 years ago by Robert Baldwin's "Great Ministry," a centre-left 1848–51 coalition of the Upper Canada Assembly, which was facing the rise of unruly burgs like Muddy York and the issue of how to control them. Baldwin's solution was to make them wards of the provinces. Over the ensuing century and a half, critical differences in the ways the provinces have exercised their powers over cities have developed. B.C.'s are arguably the most imaginative.

"WHEN I LOOK across the country," says Richard Taylor, longtime executive director of the Union of B.C. Municipalities (UBCM), "B.C. has much more of a hands-off approach to local government, and that is [true] no matter who's in power. In Quebec and Ontario, the provinces are far more interventionist in local government, period. You still have in Ontario an Ontario Municipal Board that reviews local bylaws. The provincial governments are far less interventionist in B.C., far more supportive of relationships between the region and the federal government. You don't see that elsewhere. In Quebec, there is sort of an edict: the federal government doesn't talk to municipalities. Here there's a far better respect for what people do in local government matters."

Taylor ought to know, Ken Cameron observes. "Richard has built the UBCM into one of the most influential forces in provincial politics. Attendance at the annual convention is virtually mandatory for all members of cabinet. Other MLAs and provincial officials know that co-operation with local government is an article of faith in any modern provincial administration and that the UBCM is the broker for that co-operation."

BRITISH COLUMBIANS BY and large have no idea how much freedom their cities enjoy. Nor are they aware how bountiful the fruits of that freedom have been.

Vancouver's charter is a provincial act that is essentially under the city's control. Its broad delegation of power to the city was a model for the recently adopted Community Charter for all local governments in the province. And B.C.'s system of regional districts was a provincial government idea that has worked in ways those who conceived it in the mid-1960s could never have imagined.

B.C.'s regional districts allow one way of uploading power from elected local councils. Municipalities are close to the users of such services as public transit but lack the money to buy the buses every level of government agrees we need. As services were downloaded on Canadian cities by the provinces in the 1980s and '90s, those municipalities were forced to find new, more creative ways of funding those services. Often they asked the consumer to pay. Just as often in B.C., though, the regional districts and their agencies were achieving cheaper, more efficient capital-project funding by pooling their assessed property values to get lower interest rates. They were also finding new income flows to ease the pressure on local government's traditional revenue stream, the property tax. The Municipal Finance Authority, the agency that finances capital projects as a kind of credit union for local governments in B.C., is better at what it does than the banks. Greater Vancouver has benefited from these unique B.C. solutions to local government problems.

When people think of Vancouver's setting, they think of mountains and water, the Chinese characters for which, taken together, mean the idealized, steepsided "landscape." But the City of Vancouver has other settings, too—political, economic and legal. There is a constantly shifting balance of power among Greater Vancouver's municipalities, the regional district and the provincial government. The balance is tipping in favour of the local and regional governments right now.

The executive director of Governance and Structure in the B.C. ministry of Community Affairs is Gary Paget. Asked whether his office has an enforcement function that would amount to a leash on local government, Paget replies, "Very limited. We do approve some regional district and community bylaws. It's very much an empowerment. We give them the tools and let them make decisions. We design the rules of the game, and we adjust them. We monitor and watch and are constantly changing the legislation. In the planning sphere, things have been very stable since 2000. It's pretty hard to argue that local governments need more power. The debates over the last decade have been saying that, in the planning sphere, the local governments have too much power and we have to make corrections to deal with that. That argument is largely from the development industry.

"Jurisprudence has generally gone in favour of empowerment. Supreme Court decisions, seminal,

groundbreaking decisions mostly from the Supreme
Court of Canada, such as the Arbutus Corridor, that
is, the CPR vs. Vancouver, are establishing the preroga-
tives of councils to make decisions for their communities. [The CPR owns a set of tracks and the land under
them, running from Marpole via East Boulevard to
the Molson's brewery at the south end of the Burrard
Bridge. The CPR wants to develop the right-of-way; the
City of Vancouver wants it to remain as open space.]
And then you have organizations like the Urban Development Institute pushing back, saying empowerment
has gone too far, so we've made adjustments."

"In the high-growth regions," Paget adds, "we've
been really quite instrumental in helping develop
growth strategies. A couple of the [high-growth]
regional districts, including the GVRD, have good
relationships with the province. Apart from the differences over the Pacific Gateway program and the
future of TransLink, the province and the GVRD have
co-operated over the Green Zones. The formation of
TransLink was negotiated. Some [features] the region
asked for. They had to negotiate it, and the model was
a compromise between what the province wanted and
what the GVRD wanted. It was a kind of a hybrid."

"Historically," Paget reminds us, "all of these decisions were made unilaterally by the province, B.C. Electric, then B.C. Hydro and B.C. Transit ramming Sky-
Train down the region's throat. The region didn't like

the technology, they didn't like the routes and they didn't like the stations. The TransLink debate was ugly, but at the end of the day, the government made what it thought was the right decision."

Why can't the GVRD work out the optimal solution to an issue such as rapid transit? One answer is that regional districts were designed *not* to have that kind of power. In fact they were designed with no powers and in some cases with nothing to do. Richard Taylor explains: "The GVRD is not part of a hierarchy of government that says, 'Okay, the region does this and the municipalities have to obey and fall into line.' It's a service-delivery entity. The GVRD supplies water, it supplies sewers. Its purpose is fairly benign compared with a rigid plan.

"Under the legislation the GVRD inherited from the Lower Mainland Regional Planning Board, local bylaws had to conform to the official regional plan. Ultimately, that was unacceptable. While there's some of that in the Regional Growth Strategies, [it] was based on a model where you encouraged co-operation, with consensus and conformity through negotiation and mediation." In other words, the regional district board members try to operate by getting along. Nobody has to make headlines.

"In a government structure I think the large view is that the GVRD is not a fourth level of government. The regional district is there because of and for its municipal members. The whole notion of appointing a board instead of electing a board reinforces that," Taylor says. "It's not perfect. And sometimes there is frustration between the region and the province, in that the province gets frustrated because the region can't seem to get its act together. It's this notion of trying to find agreement on the board that this is in the region's interests and municipalities should set aside their differences."

But how often does that kind of agreement happen? Right off Taylor's cuff, at least once. Vancouver and the other cities in Canada got a boost not long ago when the federal gas-tax money earmarked for local governments was set to be doled out by the provinces. "One thing that was unique about the agreement," Taylor says, "was it was the first time the UBCM, on behalf of its members, was the signatory along with Canada and B.C. Usually we're just an observer. The only other province that has such a relationship is Ontario. Premier Campbell said, 'That is federal money that is going to the municipalities, why is it coming to the province? We don't need to do this.'

"We [the UBCM] got the gas-tax money and the public transit funding, which together is $700 million. When we came to the allocation decision, the regional board directed that it all go to the Greater Vancouver Transportation Authority (TransLink).

"I was quite nervous that when municipalities realized there was $300 million [in gas-tax money] available they would say, Vancouver, we want our share, Surrey, we want our share. I think that was a remarkable example of the board setting aside local interests and saying, 'No, the biggest thing we have to do in this region is get money into transit. I'll set aside the fact that I sure could use the money for my pet projects in Surrey.'"

ABOVE ALL OTHER thresholds Vancouver has crossed to remain livable has been the democratization of politics at every level, which sometimes involves just getting the various orders of government to sit down together. Some of the region's blessings have resulted from political decisions, such as the creation of Trans-Link. Others have been unasked for, coming gift-wrapped in legal language. Such was the case with regional districts.

Regional districts are unique to British Columbia, and they have survived the trend in other provinces to create amalgamated megacities. That is partly because of their flexibility; they provide services to municipalities and electoral areas only if those entities want and are prepared to pay for them. This allows for immediate needs to be met by a coalition of the willing. Services to the larger regions then evolve over time, in tune with financial capabilities and geographic realities. Only five per cent of British Columbia is habitable, but many services have to be delivered outside those toeholds within a province that is bigger than California, Oregon and Washington State combined. A regional district can consist of several electoral areas or municipalities and is often formed so that member municipalities can specialize delivering services they are uniquely positioned to provide for themselves.

Geography is only part of the attraction of regional districts. The fact that they do not always conform to ground-based landscape features gives them the freedom to innovate in civil engineering by incorporating sustainability concepts in the requirements for new buildings, finding new ways of funding capital works or just plain pumping water from one municipality to another. In a regional district format, too, the politics are those of upward empowerment; politicians are appointed by their colleagues, the elected members of city and town councils, to entities that, taken altogether, represent almost everybody in B.C.

Another blessing from the province has been the system of assessing property market values. It took more than a hundred years for one of the most obvious sources of corruption—tax collection—to be reformed in B.C. Since the appointment of the first assessor at New Westminster in 1860, B.C. politicians have tinkered with the system's two components: the value of the property being taxed and the rate of taxation. No uniform or fair assessment system could result from the political appointment of individual assessors and assessment companies in each municipality; in 1973, for instance, there were 140 property assessment agencies in the province.

A special all-party legislative committee struck to explore the B.C. tax system in 1973 called for an independent assessment authority, duly created in mid-1974. The B.C. Assessment Authority employs the assessors and keeps them independent of the tax collection system.

Market value assessment (MVA) was long recognized as a necessary reform of the property tax system. In MVA a value is set based on market data, usually a couple of points below what a property might sell for. Appeal your assessment as being too high, and the first question the assessor or appeal body will ask is whether you would sell at that price. That question usually ends the appeal. Values can go up slowly when MVA is done annually.

The adoption of MVA leaves only the tax rate to be determined politically, depending on how much money the municipality needs. Rates can remain the same to keep pace with inflation, go down in times of lesser need or rise in times of greater need. The process is fairly easy for taxpayers to understand.

Another wildly successful tool is the Municipal Finance Authority (MFA), which has a better credit rating than the Province of Ontario, the Province of British Columbia or any of the chartered banks of

Canada. The MFA-B.C. lends money to regional districts and municipalities, ploughing its profits back into the membership. The better the institution does, the less interest taxpayers pay to finance community capital projects such as ice rinks, theatres and hospitals. The MFA has been putting up some impressive numbers since it was conceived in 1970—it has raised more than $5 billion for community capital projects. Moody's Investors Service rates MFA debt at AAA; Standard & Poor's Rating Services likes them at AA+. "This is higher than the Province of British Columbia," the MFA reports on its Web site, "whose issues are rated in the AA category by the various agencies." The high rating means the MFA can negotiate the most favourable terms for long-term borrowing requirements.

However, the powers that be help those who help themselves. Peter Oberlander's insight after the 1948 Fraser River flood was that the river was an entity as tangible as the towns and cities it ran through. It needed to be protected against upstream waste, and its adjoining municipalities and electoral areas had to be discouraged from allowing settlements on its floodplain. Some of the played-out mining towns along the Fraser, though, were hard-pressed to find the money to share responsibility for the river.

As time passed, some regional officials, including Gordon Campbell, realized that the health of the communities on the Fraser's banks greatly affected its condition. The salmon resources of the Fraser, which drains 25 per cent of B.C., were already threatened by overfishing, loss of habitat and climate change. The river's water was further degraded by toxic industrial chemicals and debris from upstream logging, mills, and pulp and paper and mining operations. As the river flowed south, it was invaded by municipal sewage, encroachment and urban runoff.

Campbell organized the Fraser Basin Management Board in 1992, as mayor of Vancouver, after an argument with the mayor of Prince George, John Backhouse, over whose city should clean up its end of the Fraser first. Campbell convened meetings of the riverside mayors to form the board; under the strategic leadership of Executive Director David Marshall and Greg Halsey-Brandt, former Richmond mayor, it morphed after its intended five-year life into the Fraser Basin Council, which is dedicated to building more sustainable communities by integrating social, economic and environmental priorities. In a precedent-setting move, the council from the outset recognized the equal legitimacy of four levels of government—federal, provincial, local and First Nations—and incorporated them in its governance structure. The council has developed more influence than ever because of the timeliness of its mission and the clout of its chairs, who have numbered among them Iona Campagnolo, B.C.'s lieutenant governor; Jack Blaney, who made Simon Fraser University

a multi-campus institution; Expo 86 director-general
Patrick Reid; and Dr. Charles Jago, former president of
the University of Northern B.C.

AN EARLY THEORIST, Arthur Maass, summarized the
currencies of government as "area and power." Getting
the two into the right relationship is the trick. Looking back over sixty years of relations between provincial and local governments in British Columbia, Ken
Cameron observes a pattern of practical evolution and
adjustment of powers and boundaries to reflect changing circumstances: "It reflects respect for local government as the creation of the people, rather than the
creature of the province, and a view that the role of the
province is to enable and empower local governments
to care for their communities. In the final analysis,
that is a far more powerful form of sovereignty than
recognition of local government in the constitution,
a goal to which municipalities in Canada have long
aspired but will never achieve."

From Livability
to Sustainability

WITHIN FOUR MONTHS in 2005, the Vancouver region won three important international city-life awards. It was named most livable city in the world (out of 127 surveyed) by the Economist Intelligence Unit, the business information arm of the *Economist* magazine. It was chosen the top North American destination for international conventions. And, for the second of three consecutive years, Condé Nast's *Traveler* magazine named Vancouver "best city in the Americas," prevailing over quaint San Miguel de Allende in Mexico and Buenos Aires.

It would be tempting to assume that the job of securing a bright future for Greater Vancouver is done. Even Gordon Price, ex-councillor, director of Simon Fraser University's City Program and one of the most thoughtful observers of public affairs in the region, says, "The short term looks great. We're in a golden age from 1986 to, minimally, 2020. Some of it is fortuitous, but you have to give some credit to the leadership. This region was built on a solid foundation from those forty years of planning. We're enjoying an extraordinarily high quality of life."

Such comments should set off alarm bells for any student of history, and they do for Ken Cameron and Mike Harcourt. "Our consensus approach to regional governance has run out of gas," Cameron says, using a politically incorrect metaphor. "Without a concerted effort to restore the ability of local and provincial governments to plan and act together with the involvement of the private sector and citizens, we will slide into the path of the poorly planned, auto-dependent, non-inclusive communities that we see elsewhere in North America."

"That's not a future that is sustainable," Harcourt adds. "We have to restore our ability to work together and apply our attention to a range of problems that threaten the fabric of our society. We have to build sustainability on our platform of livability."

Cameron agrees. "As important as the achievements of the past sixty years are," he says, "they are mainly about physical things: farmland, floodplain, neighbourhoods, transportation systems, land use. The future of a region is more than this. We must be able to chart a course that will take us towards sustainability, defined by Dr. Gro Harlem Brundtland, the former prime minister of Norway and director general of the World Health Organization, as 'development that meets the needs of the current generation without compromising the ability of future generations to meet their needs.' That means integrating the social, economic, environmental and cultural elements of our society and being focussed on local action within the context of global challenges to the future of our civilization."

Cameron and Harcourt are not alone in realizing that the focus, the direction, indeed the whole purpose of planning and decision making on the regional level must change. It is time for planners, politicians and active citizens to respond to the forces that have created permanent food banks, homelessness, marginalization of First Nations, an epidemic of property crime and a sense of helplessness in the face of Mother Nature's wrath.

The first job of government is to protect its citizens. The mission statement for the 1990 report *Creating Our Future: Steps to a More Livable Region* proposes a high standard of care and entitlement for everyone in the region, and further proposes that local government lead the way. Greater Vancouver can be, the statement said, "the first urban region in the world to combine in one place the things to which humanity aspires on a global basis"—an environment enhanced, not degraded, by human activity, where diversity of origins and religions "is a source of strength, not strife," where people control the destiny of their community, and "where the basics of food, clothing, shelter and useful activity are accessible to all." For us not to fulfill those basic needs when it is entirely possible to do so would both betray Greater Vancouver's citizens and invite history's harsh judgement.

"We know what we have to do," Harcourt says bluntly. "It's all there in any number of reports, and I've written more than my share. We just have to get off our butts and do it."

FOR KEN CAMERON, the first priority is to re-establish the close connection between regional growth management and transportation plans. "You can't provide efficient urban transportation services unless you have higher-density communities that can support transit," he asserts. "And you can't sell higher-density development without a high quality of transportation service. If your land use and transportation plans support each other, you will reduce the amount of fuel burned in transportation and space heating, which improves air quality and reduces the greenhouse gas emissions that are behind global climate change. The Livable Region Strategic Plan has been "under review" since 1991, and a lot of the region's leaders have found that it suits their purposes to dwell on the flaws of

the plan and the shortcomings of its enabling legislation. If there's something better out there, let's put it
in place. If not, let's get behind what we have and move
forward. Whatever the choice, *let's move forward*."

Mark Holland shares this sense of urgency. The
former manager of sustainability for the City of Vancouver, Holland runs a consulting firm with projects in
cities as varied as Langley, Albuquerque and Shanghai.
He believes the GVRD has the ideal geographic scope of
coverage for dealing with land-use questions. "I think
we have several very significant questions in front of
us," Holland says. "One of them, [which] will define the
viability of every square foot of development in this
region, is how we will choose to get around. And that's
where the regional scale of thinking becomes so critical. The road system is already strained." His concept is
supported by the final report of the External Advisory
Committee on Cities and Communities (From Restless
Communities to Resilient Places, www.infrastructure.
gc.ca), submitted to Prime Minister Stephen Harper
on behalf of the committee by its chair, Mike Harcourt,
in June 2006. The report recognizes the importance of
transportation to competitiveness in city-regions, particularly gateway cities such as Greater Vancouver.

Gateway cities are those that play a role in the international movement of goods and people. As part of its
effort to maximize the benefit of Canada's trade with
the fast-growing economies on the other side of the

Pacific, British Columbia has sponsored the Gateway Program of improvements to transportation facilities, designed to ensure that the flow of people and goods through Greater Vancouver is not unduly impeded by the day-to-day travel of residents of the region. Harcourt is an enthusiastic supporter of the Gateway Program, including the controversial proposal to twin the Port Mann Bridge, if it's done by giving priority to goods movement, transit and high-occupancy vehicles over solo drivers. Cameron is more cautious. "Provincial transportation priorities need to be harmonized with regional transportation priorities," he says. "If we don't do that, there is a danger that new road facilities will not only frustrate the regional objectives of denser land use and more transit, but also generate new congestion that will in turn impede the region's gateway functions. It's a classic example of the need for collaboration rather than competition. We have to be efficient in allocating scarce resources such as land and money in a way that supports broad public objectives."

The economic promise of the gateway concept is undeniable, and many feel the Greater Vancouver region and its governments would be derelict in their duty not to pursue it. It's an element of competitiveness—a concept that should drive much broader thinking about the region's economic strategy.

Except that there is no such strategy, in spite of many efforts to create one. "Municipalities in Greater

Vancouver have to realize that they are not competing with each other or even with Toronto or Montreal,"
Harcourt says. "They are competing against other
countries' big cities, particularly for the creative class
that the prime minister's Advisory Committee and
[economist and urban studies theorist] Richard Flor-
ida have identified as *the* key to economic prosperity in
an increasingly urban-based knowledge economy."

Harcourt's sentiments are echoed by Jock Finlay-
son, executive vice president of the Business Council
of B.C., who is scathing in his assessment of the priority local politicians give to economic matters. "They'd
rather spend their time talking about air quality, which
is good here, or fighting with the province," he recently
told *B.C. Business* magazine. "The local political leadership is really missing in action at the regional level
on all the items that touch on economic development."
Other private sector leaders are also trying to establish some overall direction for Greater Vancouver's
economy, which is a key driver and hub in the economy
of British Columbia as a whole.

"Once again, we know what is to be done," Harcourt
observes. "We just have to do it."

GREATER VANCOUVER CAN be justly proud of its
achievements in environmental management during
the past fifty years. The air is cleaner, the region's
waterways are less polluted and the quality of its

drinking water continues to be among the best in the world. The management plans for solid waste and liquid waste that local governments have adopted, with constructive support from federal and provincial governments, show what can be achieved for the region's commons through governments working together. The same level of co-operation needs to be applied to the remaining challenges, which relate to the excessive, inefficient consumption of non-renewable energy and its consequences in the form of air pollution and greenhouse gas emissions. "Updating and recommitting to transportation and growth management plans that support higher densities, walking, cycling and transit can take us part of the way there," Ken Cameron says, "but we need to continue strengthening our leadership role in the promotion of buildings and developments that have a greatly reduced footprint in terms of energy consumption, waste generation and water use."

If anyone knows about the potential of Greater Vancouver's leadership role in urban sustainability, it would be Nola-Kate Seymoar, president and chief executive officer of the Vancouver-based International Centre for Sustainable Cities. Seymoar's sustainability roots run deep, coming directly from Dr. Gro Harlem Brundtland's tour of North America in 1988. She was a member of the team that produced the cities-PLUS hundred-year plan for Greater Vancouver, which won the gold prize in 2003 in the International Gas Union's juried competition for sustainable urban systems design. She parlayed that success and the global attention generated by the UN-Habitat's third World Urban Forum in Vancouver in 2006 into the PLUS Network, a virtual co-operative of more than thirty cities around the world who are committed to learning from long-term planning for urban sustainability. "What we found with citiesPLUS," Seymoar says, "is that Greater Vancouver's urban systems, which seem so resilient now, would break down within about forty years. Even more important, we learned that if we take a hundred-year perspective with that knowledge, we can come up with doable strategies and actions that will help us avoid those breakdowns and create more sustainable and enriching futures for our citizens. Brundtland's challenge is to think globally and act locally. The PLUS Network allows us to develop and share practical local knowledge on a global scale. That's neat. What's even neater is the grounds that these efforts give us for optimism and hope that humanity can take the actions necessary to avert disaster for our species and other beneficial forms of life on Earth."

While Seymoar builds a global network for constructive change, Cheeying Ho has been helping connect the sustainability dots in local municipalities, sometimes described as "the Hell's Kitchen of sustainability." A member of Harcourt's External Advisory Committee on

Cities and Communities, Ho has spent thirteen years in environmental advocacy, first with the Better Environmentally Sound Transportation (BEST) society and more recently as executive director of Smart Growth B.C. BEST can claim much of the credit for having bicycling lanes established on the arterials in downtown Vancouver. With Smart Growth B.C., Ho is trying to get sustainable approaches incorporated into the plans, agendas and policies in the countless decisions made every Monday night by twenty-odd municipal councils that together will determine the shape of Greater Vancouver's future. "Councils need to be reminded, politely and constructively and by people from outside their own community, that their decisions affect a broader public interest," she says. "In playing that role, we have helped councils realize there are alternatives to sprawl and auto dependency that are better for the well-being of their own residents, too."

AS A MEMBER of the 2010 Olympic Bid Committee, Iona Campagnolo, former federal member of parliament and cabinet member and former chair of the Fraser Basin Council, was responsible for British Columbia's commitment to make the 2010 Olympic and Paralympic Games the first sustainable games. It is safe to assume that few understood the meaning of that commitment at the time. But as the games approached, it was clear what it should not mean. It should not mean people displaced from low-cost housing to make way for athletes and spectators. It should not mean 1,200 or more people sleeping on the streets in Vancouver and suburban municipalities. It should not mean a drug addiction problem that wrecks lives and feeds an epidemic of petty crime. It should not mean an international celebration that fails to acknowledge and include the Aboriginal peoples of the host jurisdiction.

After Vancouver/Whistler had won the bid, it would have been tempting to downplay or limit the sustainability component. Except that Campagnolo, famous for keeping commitments and insisting that others do likewise, was by then in a unique position—the Queen's representative as lieutenant governor of British Columbia—to convey her expectation that the commitment be fulfilled. The honour of Her Honour was at stake.

It is not, perhaps, the best reason for confronting some ugly and complicated problems, but it will do.

Judy Graves, the City of Vancouver's advocate for the homeless, is accustomed to working overnight several times a month, locating and counting the people she finds sleeping outdoors. In 2006 she initiated a program to fast-track homeless people off the street one by one, feed them breakfast and have them into their own quarters by noon of the same day. That program is now being duplicated across British Columbia as one of the recommendations of the provincial Task Force on Homelessness.

"Homelessness," Graves says, "has continued to rise every year since 1996, and it is continuing to rise. It's a seasonal thing, of course. Six hundred people slept outside on the night of Thursday, November 30, 2006. In summer, it's more than double. In Vancouver's Downtown Eastside, the shelters have been the last refuge, and on that night they maxed out. You simply can't have public order when people don't have a place to go at night."

At the core of any response, in Mike Harcourt's view, is a start on construction of 1,200 to 1,500 units of better than single-room occupancy housing by a combination of market developers and non-profit housing corporations. "More units should follow," he says, "throughout Vancouver and the Lower Mainland, instead of just in the Downtown Eastside."

Affordable housing alone won't solve the problem, Harcourt joins others in arguing. More easily accessible treatment for addicts is a necessary complement. Altogether, Harcourt says, Greater Vancouver citizens spend in the hundreds of millions of dollars a year policing and suffering the effects of the drug trade. Drug law enforcement is focussed on many people for whom a $100 increase in welfare rates would make all the difference. Instead, a "security" culture has grown up around automotive anti-theft devices, home alarm systems and rising home insurance premiums. Currently, by Harcourt's estimate, the police intercept only 2 per cent of the drugs arriving in Vancouver.

"The Swiss, the Dutch, the Brits and the Australians have all legalized recreational and certain other drugs," Harcourt points out. "If our current approach has a 2 per cent success rate, isn't it time to consider alternatives?"

Certainly, too, it would be embarrassing for the Paralympic Games to be held in a place that marginalizes the disabled. Although Harcourt has always had more than a passing interest in the need to bring people with disabilities into the mainstream of society, his own experience with disabling injuries heightened his commitment to this cause and created an opportunity to provide leadership. A practical and comprehensive agenda for action exists in the form of the *Measuring Up* guide, a blueprint produced under the auspices of 2010 Legacies Now—a body established in connection with the forthcoming Olympic and Paralympic Winter Games—for providing housing, transportation, training and employment, services and quality of life improvements for the region's disabled citizens. Again, says Harcourt, all that's needed is the political will to make that plan a reality.

A WOMAN NAMED Kwuntiltunaat may prove to be the pivotal person in calming the riptide of injustice and misery that resulted from the settlement of the lands around the Salish Sea (the Strait of Georgia) by Europeans, Asians and other newcomers. She is Kim Baird, the highly regarded chief of the Tsawwassen First Nation who led the negotiation of the first urban Aboriginal land and resource claims settlement treaty in British Columbia.

There was much to be compensated for. Their small community was fractured by two highways and a railway, and their fishing grounds were ruined by the construction of the B.C. Ferries terminal and the Roberts Bank superport in the 1960s. From a community of thousands, which for thousands of years had thrived on the salmon fishery at the mouth of what we now know as the Fraser River, Tsawwassen had declined, by the beginning of the twentieth century, to fifty or so holdouts on a 490-acre reserve. They have since rebounded to 330 people on 710 acres. But a present-day unemployment rate of 38 per cent and an average family income one third that of nearby non-Aboriginal communities were powerful incentives to seek redress.

In the long process that led to federal and provincial agreement to begin negotiations, the Tsawwassen developed outstanding political leadership. Baird had been preparing to defend what is left of her people's land and resources for almost all of her life. At twenty, she was a researcher and negotiator matched up against federal and provincial opponents. Like any good negotiator, she realized what was at stake for the other participants. The burgeoning trade between British Columbia and Asia—coal outbound and containers inbound—was creating a need for expansion of the Roberts Bank terminal and for backup lands for industrial development. The plans would require the removal of land from the Agricultural Land Reserve for industrial and port development, a virtual impossibility if viewed conventionally, but more feasible if part of a treaty settlement that delivered social justice and cleared the way for economic development. Such a scenario provided the opportunity for the Tsawwassen to be direct participants in the industrial development as well as benefiting from the new jobs that would be created on their doorstep.

Soon the deals started to roll.

In late 2004, Chief Baird concluded negotiations with the Vancouver Port Authority that earmarked $1 billion for expansion of the superport and $47 million over thirty years in compensation and jobs for the Tsawwassen—the first such deal between a First Nation and a port authority and, just as important, a deal outside the treaty process.

At about the same time, Kim Baird became only the eleventh band leader in Canada to be authorized by the federal government to manage her nation's own affairs. The capper was an agreement in principle with the federal and provincial governments on their land claim, which includes a parcel in the Agricultural Land Reserve. That made them the fourth First Nation—and the first in an urban context—to sustain their land claim in a treaty settlement.

"The implications of this agreement in an urban area are huge," Ken Cameron observes. "They involve planning and development control, servicing, transportation, you name it. The local municipality was completely unable to deal with these in any constructive way. It remains to be seen whether the GVRD can provide an appropriate context for reconciliation of the interests and objectives of the Aboriginal community with those of the Greater Vancouver region as a whole."

"Kim Baird and the Tsawwassen are the future of First Nations in this region," Mike Harcourt states emphatically. "One of our priorities now must be to achieve reconciliation and to reverse more than two hundred years of neglect and disrespect. Kim and her people have shown that they have the maturity to embark upon the healing process. Do we?"

THE REPORT OF the External Advisory Committee's on Cities and Communities suggests that there is a fourth dimension to sustainability beyond the social, economic and environmental—the cultural. "Canadians feel great pride in the places in which they live, a pride that goes beyond economic achievements, social equality, and natural wealth. Canada's cities and communities need jobs, roads, housing and schools, but their citizens also need to feel connected with each other and to enjoy a sense of shared community identity. That community identity is the basis of what we mean by culture, and our sense of who we are in our communities is our cultural identity."

The report goes on to say, "Culture is both a set of objects (art, music, theatre, buildings) and a set of processes. Culture is not just the pictures and books produced by regions and communities or nations; it is also their beliefs, their behaviour and how they develop and express them." It is this latter sense of culture that is the most important for creativity and sustainability in the long term. As well, "cultural sustainability ties together the other three dimensions, and is essential to community success."

"I think these findings have great relevance to the future of Greater Vancouver," Harcourt says. "Lower Mainland municipal leaders, cultural organizations and planners should pursue these recommendations with Canada, B.C. and other communities. We also have an opportunity to build on a new relationship with Aboriginal citizens by creating a new set of cross-cultural opportunities. These could range from a national museum of Aboriginal art with Bill Reid's work as a centrepiece to a reconciliation and rejoice event as part of B.C.'s 2008 150th-anniversary celebrations. We should expand on the tremendous progress on multicultural diversity as a source of the Vancouver area's strength and appeal as not only one of the world's most livable cities, but one of the most sustainable."

"One of the most endearing qualities of humans is the attachment they form to the place in which they live, no matter how modest it may seem to others," Ken Cameron observes. "But I believe the residents of Greater Vancouver have an even stronger attachment to, and pride in, the paradise in which they have the good fortune to live. The air is like a caress, the water is like fine wine, the landscape is drop-dead gorgeous, the design of public and private spaces is outstanding, and the people are building a tolerant, compassionate society like nowhere else on Earth. I love the place, and I think it can offer a beacon of hope to those who think human beings can live in peace with each other and with Mother Nature. Could there be a nobler task for the leaders of today and tomorrow?"

Harcourt agrees, returning to his main theme. "We know what to do. Let's do it."

Sources and Recommended Reading

Asterisks indicate sources consulted
during the writing of this book.

BOOKS

*Alan Artibise and Michael Seelig. *From Desolation to Hope: The Pacific Fraser Region in 2010* (Vancouver: University of British Columbia Press, 1991).

Dave Barrett and William Miller. *Barrett: A Passionate Political Life* (Vancouver: Douglas & McIntyre, 1995). Political memoirs of the most productive premier in B.C. history.

*Pierre Berton. *Adventures of a Columnist* (Toronto: McClelland and Stewart, 1960). Contains Berton's reflections on his hometown of Vancouver in the fifties.

*Chuck Davis, ed. *The Greater Vancouver Book* (Vancouver: Linkman Press, 1997). A one-stop source of facts about Vancouver and environs.

A.L. Farley. *Atlas of British Columbia: People, Environment and Resource Use* (Vancouver: UBC Press, 1979).

*Daniel Francis, ed. *Encyclopedia of British Columbia* (Madeira Park, B.C.: Harbour Publishing, 2000).

*Catherine Gourley. *Island in the Creek: The Granville Island Story* (Madeira Park, B.C.: Harbour Publishing/Aldrich/ Pears Associates, 1988).

*Donald Gutstein. *Vancouver Ltd.* (Toronto: James Lorimer & Company Publishers, 1975). Excellent coverage of the urban renewal and freeway fights in Strathcona.

Mike Harcourt with Wayne Skene. *Mike Harcourt: A Measure of Defiance* (Vancouver: Douglas & McIntyre, 1996).

*Walter G. Hardwick. *Vancouver* (Toronto: Collier-Macmillan Canada, 1974). Insights into Vancouver's all-too-brief reform era and the beginnings of public participation in planning issues.

*Bruce Hutchison. *The Fraser* (Toronto: Clarke, Irwin & Co. Ltd., 1950). Still the best book on the subject; includes an account of the 1948 flood.

*Harry Lash. *Planning in a Human Way* (Ottawa: Urban Prospects Series, Ministry of State for Urban Affairs, 1976). A handbook for public participation in planning decisions. Rare but available via the Web.

*Bruce Macdonald. *Vancouver: A Visual History* (Vancouver: Talonbooks, 1992). A decade-by-decade pictorial and map-based account of Vancouver's development.

Robert A.J. McDonald. *Making Vancouver, 1863–1913* (Vancouver: UBC Press, 2000 ed.). Vancouver from just after European contact to the end of the greatest boom the city has ever known, 1907–12.

˙ James H. Marsh, ed. *The Canadian Encyclopedia* (Edmonton: Hurtig Publishers Ltd., 1988). With five pages, starting at p. 2227, on urban and regional planning, citizens' movements and urban design.

˙ Judy Oberlander. "History of Planning in Greater Vancouver" from *The Greater Vancouver Book* (Vancouver: Linkman Press, 1997). Also on the Web at www.discovervancouver. com/gvb/vancouver-history-planning.asp.

Kris Olds. "Canada: Hallmark Events, Evictions, and Housing Rights," in A. Azuela, E. Duhau and E. Ortiz, eds. *Evictions and the Right to Housing* (Ottawa: International Development Research Centre, 1998).

˙ John Punter. *The Vancouver Achievement: Urban Planning and Design* (Vancouver: UBC Press, 2003). The best book-length account of planning and building Vancouver from 1972 to the present.

˙ Ted Rashleigh. *A Documentary Review of the Livable Region Plan, 1970–75* (Burnaby: GVRD, 1997). A compilation of reports, memos, meeting notes and other documents relating to the Livable Region Plan, available for reference use at the GVRD Harry Lash Library.

REPORTS AND ARTICLES

Elizabeth Aird. "Municipal Politicians Off on the Wrong Track," *Vancouver Sun*, January 30, 1998.

B.C. Land Commission. *Keeping the Options Open* (Victoria: B.C. Land Commission, 1975).

˙Charles Campbell. *Forever Farmland: Reshaping the Agricultural Land Reserve for the 21st Century* (Vancouver: David Suzuki Foundation, 2006).

Narissa Anne Chadwick. *Regional Planning in British Columbia: 50 Years of Vision, Process and Practice*, Master's thesis, April 2002.

˙Shirley Y. Chan. *An Overview of the Strathcona Experience with Urban Renewal by a Participant* (Ottawa: Action Research, Secretary of State Department, 1971). An invaluable inside account of the freeway and urban renewal fights in Strathcona. Copy available at Vancouver City Archives.

citiesPLUS. *A Sustainable Urban System: The Long-Term Plan For Greater Vancouver* (Vancouver: Sheltair Group, 2003).

˙City of Vancouver. *Vancouver Redevelopment Study* (Vancouver: City of Vancouver, 1958).

˙Tony Eberts. "Freeway: Concrete Knife in the Heart of Chinatown?," *Province*, December 2, 1967.

Bud Elsie. "Oberlander Resigns over Freeway Plan," *Vancouver Sun*, December 8, 1967.

˙External Advisory Committee on Cities and Communities. *From Restless Communities to Resilient Places: Building a Stronger Future for All Canadians* (Ottawa: Infrastructure Canada, 2006).

Brian Fawcett, Kent Gerecke and Ted Rashleigh. "The Livable Region: Three Accounts of Progress," *City Magazine,* Summer–Fall 1992.

Greater Vancouver Regional District. *Creating Our Future: Steps to a More Livable Region* (Burnaby: GVRD, 1990).

Greater Vancouver Regional District. *Livable Region Strategic Plan* (Burnaby: GVRD, 1996).

Greater Vancouver Regional District. *Transport 2021 Medium and Long Range Plans* (Burnaby: GVRD, 1993).

˙"Huge Growth Brings Issues: 1.5 Million People Could 'Strangle' Lower Mainland," *Vancouver Sun,* January 8, 1952. Analysis of first LMRPB report, *The Lower Mainland Looks Ahead.*

"Land Bill Hits Fierce Opposition," *Province,* February 23, 1973.

Lower Mainland Regional Planning Board. *Chance and Challenge: A Concept and Plan for the Development of the Lower Mainland Region* (Vancouver: LMRPB, 1963).

˙Lower Mainland Regional Planning Board. *Official Regional Plan* (Vancouver: LMRPB, 1966).

* Pete McMartin. "A Fair to Remember: The Legacy of Expo," *Vancouver Sun*, April 27, 1996.

Colleen Hardwick Nystedt. "Walter Hardwick Was My Father." Memoir of life with Hardwick written by his daughter for his memorial service June 28, 2006.

Andrew Petter. "Sausage Making in British Columbia: The Creation of the Land Commission Act, August 1972–April 1973," *B.C. Studies* no. 65, Spring 1985.

* "Regional Planning for Fraser Valley's Future: Whether It Will Be Chaos or Order Has to Be Decided Now," *Vancouver Sun*, March 15, 1952.

* Sightline Institute and Smart Growth B.C. *Sprawl and Smart Growth in Greater Vancouver: A Comparison of Vancouver, British Columbia, with Seattle, Washington* (Vancouver: Sightline Institute and Smart Growth B.C., 2002).

* Smart Growth B.C. *Gateway Program*, 2005 Annual report (Vancouver: Smart Growth B.C., 2005).

* Paul Tennant and Dave Zirnhelt. "Metropolitan Government in Vancouver: The Strategy of Gentle Imposition," *Canadian Public Administration*, Spring 1973.

James W. Wilson. "Regional Planning in British Columbia." *Community Planning Review*, November 1952.

* James W. Wilson. *The Lower Mainland's Regional Plan: A Retrospective Introduction* (Vancouver: LMRPB, 1988).

Wilson surveys the state of infrastructure in Greater Vancouver as the LMRPB was getting underway in 1950, from the vantage point of 1988, when this document was written. In the SFU collection, document F-132-1-0-0-1.

OTHER MEDIA

Greater Vancouver Regional District video tape. *Planning in a Human Way.* Harry Lash and the Livable Region Program, 1970–75. Prepared by Ted Rashleigh and Howard Harding, 1997.

"Mary Lee Chan: Taking on City Hall" in documentary series *Mother Tongue: A Woman's History of Ethnic Canada.* Written, directed and produced by Susan Poizner, copyright Think-Stock Inc. (no date given).

Acknowledgements

MUCH OF *City Making in Paradise* is based on the first-hand experiences of the authors in civic, regional and provincial affairs, and the book's themes reflect our personal perspectives on governance and leadership in the Greater Vancouver region. A great many other people, however, either made publishing this book possible or had a significant influence on its point of view.

Neither this book nor many of the achievements chronicled within it would have been possible without our spouses, Becky Harcourt, Shirley Cameron and Terri Wershler, and their fierce loyalty, unflinching honesty and extraordinary forebearance. They were the first readers of many parts of this book, and their feedback saved us from many embarrassments and future readers from much pap and foolishness.

Barbara Pulling, our editor, challenged us with well-reasoned, meticulously documented and constructive suggestions for making this a better book with broader appeal. John Lefebvre underwrote the research and editorial tasks, and we offer our sincere thanks to him for making everything else possible.

Rick Antonson of Tourism Vancouver was a much-needed early source of the encouragement that is so characteristic of him. Publisher Scott McIntyre immediately saw the possibilities of Mike Harcourt and Ken Cameron's outline for a book that was, at the concept stage, about "Vancouverism." Nola-Kate Seymoar, president and chief executive officer of the International Centre for Sustainable Cities, oversaw the project's research and writing budget and offered her insights into Vancouver's future possibilities. James Hoggan offered his connections and suggestions when *City Making* was in its formative stages. Colleen Nystedt was the source and advocate for the seminal thoughts of her father, Walter Hardwick, whose place in both the developmental history of Greater Vancouver and the post-secondary education system in British Columbia has yet to be fully appreciated—except by those who knew or worked with him.

Almost everyone we spoke with during the writing of *City Making* had strong opinions on what the book should say. Among those whose contributions we solicited but sometimes didn't have room to quote include, in alphabetical order: Kim Baird, Dave Barrett, Shirley Chan, Maurice Egan, Michael Geller, Judy Graves, David Hardwick, Cheeying Ho, Mark Holland, Betsy Lane, Darlene Marzari, Brenda Norris, Peter Oberlander, Gary Paget, Gordon Price, George Puil, Ted Rashleigh, Patrick Reid, Jim Robson, Ray Spaxman, Richard Taylor, Bob Williams and Jim Wilson. Tom Osdoba, director of the City of Vancouver's Sustainability Unit, drew the big sustainability picture of Vancouver while being interviewed for another project.

The foundations upon which a book such as this are built are the archivists, in this case the Greater Vancouver Regional District's corporate secretary, Paulette Vetleson, and its Harry Lash Library staff, Annette Dignan and Thora Gislason. The availability of published material from the GVRD enabled the creation of the maps that are included in the book.

Index

About the Authors

MIKE HARCOURT is a former premier of British Columbia, mayor of Vancouver and city councillor. He was chair of the prime minister's External Advisory Committee for Cities and Communities, which handed in its report in June 2006, and is currently honorary chair of the International Centre for Sustainable Cities and co-chair of the International Panel of Advisors. He received the Woodrow Wilson Award for Public Service in 2005 and the Canadian Urban Institute's Jane Jacobs Lifetime Achievement Award in 2006. In 2007 he was the Walter Bean Visiting Professor on the Environment at the University of Waterloo. He is also the author of two books: *Mike Harcourt: A Measure of Defiance* (with Wayne Skene) and *Plan B: One Man's Journey from Tragedy to Triumph* (with John Lekich).

KEN CAMERON'S thirty-six-year career in provincial and local government service has consistently focussed on the role of urban regions in meeting human needs sustainably. In the 1970s, he served as executive assistant to Ontario Treasurer John White and as executive director of the Royal Commission on Metropolitan Toronto headed by the late John Robarts. After returning to Vancouver in 1978, he held senior planning and management positions with the City of New Westminster and the Greater Vancouver Regional District, ultimately as manager of policy and planning. Cameron is currently CEO of the Homeowner Protection Office, a provincial Crown corporation with a mandate to enhance consumer protection for buyers of new homes in British Columbia and to bring about continued improvement in the quality of residential construction.

SEAN ROSSITER wrote an award-winning column about civic affairs entitled "Twelfth & Cambie" for *Vancouver* magazine for thirteen years. He has also written extensively on architecture and city life for *The Georgia Straight*. Rossiter has won two City of Vancouver Heritage Awards and shared another. He is the author of twenty books.